Dancing on Mountains

Kathy Keay read English and Education at Oxford and worked as a freelance writer, editor and journalist, giving workshops and seminars in the UK, the USA, India and Africa.

Rowena Edlin-White graduated in English and Drama and spent a number of years working in the theatre and television. She is a freelance writer specializing in gender issues and a published children's author.

Dancing on Mountains

an anthology of women's spiritual writings

COMPILED BY
KATHY KEAY AND ROWENA EDLIN-WHITE

HarperCollins*Publishers*

HarperCollins*Religious*
Part of HarperCollins*Publishers*
77–85 Fulham Palace Road, London W6 8JB

First published in Great Britain
in 1996 by HarperCollins

1 3 5 7 9 10 8 6 4 2

A catalogue record for this book is
available from the British Library

Hardback 0–551–03030–5
Paperback 0–551–02922–6

Printed and bound in Great Britain by
HarperCollinsManufacturing, Glasgow

For all those whose lives were touched by
KATHY KEAY
1954–1994

Contents

Obstacles

Risktaking

Climbing

Standing Together

Struggle

Wilderness

Reflection

Introduction

I have named this anthology *Dancing on Mountains*, for in the midst of life's demands, there are always moments to celebrate; historic and often incidental moments of breakthrough, breathtaking, inspiring and energizing, when the Spirit enlivens the commonplace, making us want to 'whoopee' and dance. But these moments come and go, and are usually punctuated by ordinariness, when nothing spectacular happens, and life's struggles continue. This anthology includes material which encompasses those inspiring, breathtaking moments as well as reflecting life's ordinariness and struggle, for together they constitute the raw material of our lives, nurtured by our togetherness and fed by our dreaming.

Kathy Keay, Bristol, March 1994

Kathy planned *Dancing on Mountains* as a companion volume to *Laughter, Silence and Shouting*, her beautiful collection of women's prayers. Tragically she died only months after writing the above and it was left to me to organize and augment the material she had collected, to bring this book to birth. It has been a bitter-sweet task undertaken somewhat reluctantly for a dear friend – something akin to finishing a piece of embroidery or tapestry for someone else. However, it was not difficult to catch her vision for the unfinished work, which progresses rather like a journey, a pilgrimage of life and endeavour, closely mirroring Kathy's own. She often wrote messages to herself on the poems and snippets of prose which caught her imagination. These have been produced and stand witness to the encouragement and inspiration she received from other women's writing during her last journey.

Kathy and I are similar in being incorrigible beachcombers and collectors of colourful bits and pieces, old and new, which we would store away for future use. I have dipped into my own rag-bag of precious fragments and added to Kathy's those I know she'd like and approve of.

Here then is our collection of writing by women of all ages, times, conditions and countries, expressing their spirituality through the minutiae of their everyday lives and through the unbridled possibilities of their dreams; women religious, lay women, professional women and homemakers, partnered and single women, women on the doorstep of life and women approaching the 'final passage-way'; some well known, many hitherto unknown but all with voices which deserve to be heard, which we believe will speak to you in season, inspire and energize you, encourage and comfort you on your own journey.

Rowena Edlin-White, Nottingham, October 1995

Dreaming

God's Dance of Creation

In our quest for God,
we think too much,
reflect too much.
Even when we look
at the dance we call creation
we are all the time
thinking,
analysing.
Words.
Noise.

Be silent
and contemplate the Dance.
Just look.
A star,
a flower,
a fading leaf,
a bird,
a stone
– any fragment will do.

INDIA

Come Spirit

Sing, my soul, a Spirit song,
calling all to sing along.
Fill the world with joyful sounds:
God is here and grace abounds.

Come, Spirit, come and be a new reality.
Your touch is guarantee of love alive in me.

Dance, my heart, at your rebirth,
partner to the dance of earth.
Thirsting spirit, drink your fill:
love goes dancing where it will.

Come, Spirit, come and be a new reality.
Your touch is guarantee of love alive in me.

When constrained by thoughts or things,
hear the word the Spirit brings:
life is larger than it seems,
hope is the harbinger of dreams.

Come, Spirit, come and be a new reality.
Your touch is guarantee of love alive in me.

MIRIAM THERESE WINTER

Lord of Creation

Lord of Creation,
moulder of our fragile clay,
Shape us in your image.
Spin us round if you must
until we're dizzy;
Hollow us out, if you must,
until we're empty
of all that is false and useless.
Fill us daily with living water
that we may carry your life
to a world dying of thirst.

SHEILA CASSIDY

A Handful of Clay

From a handful of clay
the black woman
(seven day's work)
Makes, in seven minutes,
her handful of clay
into an unsatisfactory bowl

She pushes it down,
sets the wheel spinning
and raises up a pot
curved, in her own image

The wheel stops, and the black woman
cuts the pot from the base
She marks the bottom with a broad thumb print
and puts the pot on one side
and grins at me
God has put her thumb print
on the black woman

FLORA WINFIELD

A Twinkle in God's Eye

Before creation was made the Vision was a twinkle in God's eye, and He/She laughed with delight as He/She thought of the joy, the colour and the music of the original idea. Part of the idea was the beauty of sex, the wonder of pro-creation, and the sacrament of mutual priesthood that each should minister to the other in order that man and woman should become One in Christ. This mutual interdependence was part of the plan ensuring that everyone should be engaged in the activity of loving.

You and I may come down to earth with a bump and say, 'It's all very well but the world is in a ripe mess just now.' Yet the Vision which was there before time began, and is the final reality which waits to be manifested, can be unexpectedly encountered when we see the Risen Christ at the traffic lights on the corner of the road. The Vision is timeless, already existing in Christ and always available for us to experience when we open ourselves and expand to take it in. We have to face the unnerving demand of planting heaven here and now in the middle of hell.

PHOEBE WILLETTS

The Womb of God

You lie within the womb of time
Kicking to break free,
To find release from the dull routine
Of feeding, loving, living.
The heart beats a note of urgency
As you push so hard
As if against stone.
Yet you do not move:
Is it still not time?
What is it that prevents you
From reaching this ecstatic freedom
For which you long so much?

You are enclosed within this womb of mine
And must wait patiently,
For it is I who have made you
And it is I who pulsates you to maturity
And so from birth to freedom.

KATHY KEAY

Birth

A cry in dark void –
Uncomprehendable, gone –
Free, my word finds flesh.

HEBE WELBOURNE

Spirit, Silken Thread

Spirit, silken thread,
Lightly wind
Through the fingers
Of my soul
She is blind.

MARGOT RUDDOCK (1907–51)

Dreaming

When vexed with waking thought, and its dull gleam,
   I – waiting on the shore of Time – oft close
   Mine eyes, and while the ocean ebbs and flows
Around me, hear its murmurous voice, and dream.
And sometimes dreaming thus, the Will supreme
   My thoughts have bent beneath, will seem to be
   A Will, not working by its sole decree,
But one that wrestles with a counter-stream.

And dreaming thus, my heart will give a bound
   Of yearning love, and wake me with a cry;
   Oh for the feet of Hermes that I might –
A chartered messenger – spurn back the ground
   And through the reeling world be charged to fly,
   With but one word to help Him in the fight.

EMILY PFEIFFER (1841–90)

O Taste and See

The world is
not with us enough
O taste and see

the subway Bible poster said,
meaning *The Lord*, meaning
if anything all that lives
to the imagination's tongue,

grief, mercy, language,
tangerine, weather, to
breathe them, bite,
savour, chew, swallow, transform

into our flesh our
deaths, crossing the street, plum, quince,
living in the orchard and being

hungry, and plucking
the fruit.

DENISE LEVERTOV

The Other

Whatever I find if I search will be wrong.
I must wait: sternest trial of all, to sit
Passive, receptive, and patient, empty
Of every demand and desire, until
That other, that being I never would have found
Though I spent my whole life in the quest, will step
From the shadows, approach like a wild, awkward child.

And this will be the longest task: to attend,
To open myself. To still my energy
Is harder than to use it in any cause.
Yet surely she will only be revealed
By pushing against the grain of my nature
That always yearns for choice. I feel it painful
And strong a birth in which there is no pause.

I must hold myself back from every lure of action
To let her come closer, a wary smile on her face,
One arm lifted – to greet me or ward off attack
(I cannot decipher that uncertain gesture).
I must even control the pace of my breath
Until she has drawn her circle near enough
To capture the note of her faint reedy voice.

And then as in dreams, when a language unspoken
Since times before childhood is recalled
(When I was as timid as she, my forgotten sister —
Her presence my completion and reward),
I begin to understand, in fragments, the message
She waited so long to deliver. Loving her I shall learn
My own secret at last from the words of her song.

RUTH FAINLIGHT

A Pilgrim's Song

Life be in my speech,
Sense in what I say,
The bloom of cherries on my lips,
Till I come back again.

The love Christ Jesus gave
Be filling every heart for me,
The love Christ Jesus gave
Filling me for every one.

Traversing corries, traversing forests,
Traversing valleys long and wild,
The fair white Mary still uphold me,
The Shepherd Jesu be my shield.
  The fair white Mary still uphold me,
  The Shepherd Jesu be my shield.

CARMINA GADELICA

First Steps

Old Indian Saying

When you were born, you cried and the world
    rejoiced.
Live your life in such a manner that when you die
the world cries and you rejoice.

Baptism by the Knee-Woman*

A small drop of water
To thy forehead, beloved,
Meet for Father, Son and Spirit,
The Triune of power.

A small drop of water
To encompass my beloved,
Meet for Father, Son and Spirit,
The Triune of power.

A small drop of water
To fill thee with each grace,
Meet for Father, Son and Spirit,
The Triune of power.

CARMINA GADELICA

*In the Highlands and Islands of Scotland it used to be customary for the baby's
'first' baptism to be conducted by the knee-woman or midwife.

A Mother's Prayer for Her Daughter's Baptism

Eternal God, you fill the heights above;
Send down your blessing now.
Remember the child of my body
In the name of the God of peace.
When the minister of your gospel
On *Esther* sprinkles the water of meaning
Give to her the blessing of the Three
who fill the heights,
The blessing of the Three
who fill the heights.

Sprinkle down upon her your grace,
Give to her virtue and growth,
Give to her strength and guidance,
Give to her faith and purity,
Sense and reason free from bitterness,
The wisdom of the angels in her day,
So that she may stand free of blame
before your throne,
So that she may stand free of blame
before your throne.

BASED ON AN ANCIENT CELTIC PRAYER

MAGGIE ELDRIDGE-MROTZEK

An Icon of Christ's Baptism

Sudden Silence.
The dove drops from a gold sky
And John's destiny is fulfilled.
Almighty God is shown,
Leaving his power and glory in the water,
Stepping forth, small and naked,
To cast his lot with his friends
Who, at this moment
On the fringe of the desert,
Are represented by angels.
They will accomplish his destiny.
But Almighty God, eternally in all things,
Shines through incarnate, as
Fish in green water and
Golden light.

HEBE WELBOURNE

Midsummer Night's Dream

But so deep the wild-bee hummeth,
And so still the glow-worm glows,
That we know a Saviour cometh,
And we lay our hearts with those –
All the mysteries earth strives with through the June nights and the
  rose.

Strange the joy that sets us weeping –
Holy John, thy Feast is come!
Yea, we feel a Babe is leaping
In the womb where he is dumb
To the song that God's own Mother sings so loud to Christendom.

High that singing, high and humble!
Lo, our Queen is taking rule:
Faint midsummer thunders rumble,
And gold lilies light the pool,
While the generations whisper that a Queen is taking rule.

MICHAEL FIELD

(KATHERINE HARRIS BRADLEY 1846-1913 & EDITH EMMA COOPER 1862–1914)

Moel Famau

Years ago I lived beneath a mountain. Its name in Welsh meant 'mother'. I clung to her broody side for four years, learning to break the hard earth, knowing the joy and frustration of bringing to birth the things that struggled in the dry dust; digging with my fingers, burrowing for meaning, for a spiritual dimension, sure of something hidden there. And the hard earth broke me, ground me down with sorrow and despair.

But now I know the Source of the pulse that throbs in the deep soil, the Breath that created every green thing, the heart at the centre of life:

'For since the creation of the world God's invisible qualities – eternal power and divine nature – have been clearly seen, being understood from what has been made . . .'

So. That's what it was that compelled me then, looking up into my face and shouting, 'See Me! Understand!'

Adam came from dust, but Eve feels the greater affinity; birth, rebirth and breaking down are mirrored in her own body, where the blood and hormones variably sing throughout her life, ebbing, flowing, holding, letting go. Little wonder I am transfixed by the geraniums in my window-box, admiring each new bud, mourning each dead leaf: we are insolubly in sympathy with one another.

ROWENA EDLIN-WHITE

A Little Blind Girl

Sometimes I rose at dawn and stole into the garden while the heavy dew lay on the grass and flowers. Few know what joy it is to feel the roses pressing softly into the hand, or the beautiful motion of the lilies as they sway in the morning breeze. Sometimes I caught an insect in the flower I was plucking and I felt the faint noise of a pair of wings rubbed together in a sudden terror, as the little creature became aware of the pressure from without. Another favourite haunt of mine was the orchard, where the fruit ripened early in July. The large downy peaches would reach themselves into my hand and as the joyous breezes flew about the trees, the apples tumbled at my feet. Oh the delight with which I gathered up the fruit into my pinafore, pressed my face against the smooth cheeks of the apples, still warm from the sun, and skipped back to the house!

HELEN KELLER (1880–1968)

Helen Keller was not only blind but profoundly deaf from an early age.

Discovery

When Mother talked of the present, however, bringing her sense of wondrous contemplation to the ordinary world we knew, we listened, feeling the mystery and the magic. She had only to say of any commonplace object, 'Look, kiddies, a stone' to fill that stone with a wonder as if it were a holy object. She was able to imbue every insect, blade of grass, flower, the dangers and grandeurs of weather and the seasons, with a memorable importance along with a kind of uncertainty and humility that led us to ponder and try to discover the heart of everything.

FROM *TO THE IS-LAND*

JANET FRAME

In our attempts to rationalize and analyse all that happens to us, we can miss the mystery and magic which gives life its deepest meaning, and us the greatest enjoyment of it.

Lord of the Universe

Lord of the Universe,
Word of Life,
open to us
the riches of your teaching.
Lead us ever deeper
into the mystery
of who you are
and where you are leading us.
Spirit of God,
open our hearts
to the wonders
of your law.

SHEILA CASSIDY

Orders for an Anchoress

First go to the water, any water:
brook, river, lake or sea, all speak
incessantly in tongues of liquid eloquence

Sit blind on bank or shore
face tipped to the wind, the sun
basting you like a baked stone

Hear the great swell wash and pull
the small stream chuckle and chattering

Rock till you too are wave
flesh flowing into the tide's sway

Run, run with the eddy's course
drench loose in the breaker's flail and shout

and then
swing still

and when your soul's swirl
balances
go

the living water's pulse in your blood

VERONICA ZUNDEL

The Beckoning Counts

The beckoning counts, and not the clicking of the latch behind you: and
all through life the actual moment of emancipation still holds that
delight, of the whole world coming to meet you like a wave.

FREYA STARK (1893–1993)

Take My Life

Take my life, and let it be
Consecrated, Lord, to Thee.
Take my moments and my days;
Let them flow in ceaseless praise.

Take my hands, and let them move
At the impulse of Thy love.
Take my feet, and let them be
Swift and beautiful for Thee.

Take my voice, and let me sing
Always, only, for my King.
Take my lips, and let them be
Filled with messages from Thee.

Take my silver and my gold;
Not a mite would I withhold.
Take my intellect, and use
Every power as Thou shalt choose.

Take my will, and make it Thine;
It shall be no longer mine.
Take my heart – it is Thine own;
It shall be Thy royal throne.

Take my love; my Lord I pour
At Thy feet its treasure-store.
Take myself, and I will be
Ever, only, all for Thee.

FRANCES RIDLEY HAVERGAL (1836–79)

The Gate of the Year

And I said to the man who stood at the gate of the year:
'Give me a light, that I may tread safely into the unknown!'
And he replied:
'Go into the darkness and put your hand in to the Hand of God.
That shall be to you better than light and safer than a known way.'
So, I went forth, and finding the Hand of God, trod gladly into the night.
And he led me towards the hills and the breaking of day in the lone East.

So, heart, be still!
What need our little life,
Our human life, to know,
If God hath comprehension?
In all the dizzy strife
Of things both high and low
God hideth His intention.

MINNIE LOUISE HASKINS (1875–1957)

I Thank Thee, O Lord

I thank Thee, O Lord, because never once in my life have I been unheard in what I feared, when I have approached Thee in a full sense of my own impotence of mind, with humility and sincerity to implore Thy divine assistance. I set to my seal that Thou art true, since I have ever found Thee so. Forbid that I should venture upon any business without first begging Thy direction and assistance. So do Thou set a check upon my mind when I would do anything that I know to be unlawful or dubious, and encourage me with hopes of success in my lawful undertakings.

Amen.

SUSANNA WESLEY (1669–1742)

Obstacles

They Call Me Woman

Dear God
They call me woman:
they blame me
for the first sin of lost innocence.
They call me Eve.

Dear God
They call me woman:
they tell me
I bore your son
who should have saved the world.
They call me Mary.

Dear God
They call me woman:
they show me
a great sinner
reconciled, forgiven,
by her love allowed to be first.
They call me Magdalen.

Dear God
They call me woman:
they send me
from your table – unworthy
from your presence – unclean
from your life – unable.

Dear God
I am woman:
worthy of you
cleansed by you
able through you.
Make me glad
when they call me woman.

CHARLOTTE METHUEN

I Am a Woman

I am a woman
  I am alive
    I am struggling
      I am hoping.

I am created in the image of God
just like all other people in the world.
I am a person with worth and dignity.
I am a thinking person, a feeling person, a doing person.
I am the small *I am* that stands before the big I AM.

I am a worker who is constantly challenged and faced
  with the needs of the Church and society in Asia
  and in the global community.

I am angered by the structures and powers that create
  all forms of oppression, exploitation, and degradation.
I am a witness of the moans, tears, banners and
  clenched fists of my people.
I can hear their liberating songs, their hopeful prayers, and decisive
  march towards justice and freedom.

I believe that all of us – women and men,
  young and old, Christian and non-Christian
  are called upon to do responsible action;
  to be concerned
  to be involved
  NOW!

I am hoping
  I am struggling
    I am alive
      I am Filipino
        I am a woman.

ELIZABETH TAPIA

At the Table of Life

We share
most disproportionally indeed.
Some go hungry,
others are besottedly full.
The quality of rice we eat is
according to the wealth or penury we bring
with us to the table.
We embarrass the poor
outrageously.

This is our world.
A world of plenty and want,
of staggering riches
and even more staggering poverty.
And into this confused
and confusing world comes
the Stranger
seeking to pitch his tent
among us.

PHILIPPINES

Give Us Today

Give us today the food we need.
Forgive us the wrongs we have done,
as we forgive the wrongs that others have done us.

MATTHEW 6:11–12

Take the Time

Take the time to sing a song
for all those people who don't belong:
for the women wasted by defeat,
the men condemned to walk the street,
the down and out we'll never meet.

Take the time to say a prayer
for all those people who face despair:
the starving multitudes who pray
to make it through another day,
who watch their children slip away.

Take the time to hear the plea
of every desperate refugee:
the millions who have had to flee
their lands, their loves, their liberty,
who turn in hope to you and me.

Take the time to take a stand
for peace and justice in every land.
Where power causes deep unrest,
come, take the part of the oppressed,
and then, says God, you will be blessed.

MIRIAM THERESE WINTER

Caribbean Woman Prayer

Wake up Lord
brush de sunflakes from yuh eye
back de sky a while Lord
and hear dis Mother-woman
on behalf of her pressure-down people

God de Mudder
God de Fadder
God de Sister
God de Brudder
God de Holy Fire

Ah don't need to tell yuh
how tings stan
cause right now you know
dat old lizard ah walk
lick land
and you know how de pickney belly laang
an you know how de fork ah hit stone
an tho it rain you know it really drought
an even now de man have start fuh count

de wata he make

God de Fadder
God de Mudder
God de Sister
God de Brudder
God de Holy Fire

Give me faith

O Lord
you know we is ah people
of a proud an generous heart
and how it shame us bad
dat we kyant welcome friend or stranger
when eat time comes around

You know is not we nature
to behave like yard fowl

You know dat is de politics
an de times
an de tricks
dat has reduced we to dis

An talking bout politics Lord
I hope you give de politicians dem
de courage to do what they have to do
an to mek dem see dat tings must grow
from within
an not from without
even as you suffer us not
to walk in de rags of doubt

Mek dem see dat de people
must be at de root of de heart
dat sis place ain't Uncle Sam backyard
Lord, look how Rodney and Bishop get blast

God de Mudder
God de Fadder
God de Sister
God de Brudder
God de Holy Fire

To cut a laang story short
I want to see de children
wake up happy to de sunrise
an food in de pot

I want to see dem stretch limb
an watch dem sleep pon good stomach
I want to see de loss of hope
everywhere replace
wid de win of living

I want to see de man an woman
being in they being

Yes Lord
Halleliuh Lord!

All green tings an hibiscus praises Lord

GRACE NICHOLS

Unnatural Selection

I have become
an independent woman.
By process of unnatural selection
I have had to learn to
be alone, live alone, and work alone.
Every month
for 26 years
I have bled out my fertility
until there is nothing left.
Now I live life from
a different orbit:
From the womb of silence
I struggle to create
a different heritage
and I am at peace.

I have become
an independent woman
who has learnt by a process of unnatural selection
to find rest in retreat
and richness in solitude,
This is who I am.
Please God
after such a painful process
don't ask me now to change.

KATHY KEAY

Surviving the Commercial Calendar

Dear God,

Surviving the Commercial Calendar has become, for some of us, a major exercise. Christmas suffocated with tinsel and rampant commercialism; Valentine's Day followed hotly by Mother's Day. Then it's Easter, the time when some of us would actually like to celebrate more but that's usually pretty low key. Father's Day, for all fatherless children, another blow, then round we come again to holidays.

When is it possible to take a break and not be reminded of all the gaps in our life?

Yours, Staunchly Avoiding All Newsagents, Corina.

FROM *LETTERS FROM A SOLO SURVIVOR*
KATHY KEAY

Love Song

Though to think
Rejoiceth me,
Love I will
Not think of Thee.

Though thy heart's
My resting place
Yet I will
Not seek embrace.

Not till soul
Has shed her pain
Will I come
To Thee again.

And then when
My heart is free
I will give
It back to Thee.

MARGOT RUDDOCK
(1907–51)

A Mother is a Person

a mother is a person
who gives birth
cleans up messes
kisses dirty faces
makes thousands of peanut butter sandwiches
and says no more often than yes

a mother is a person
who acts as chauffeur
personal secretary
and general contractor
housebreaks and feeds the dog
hunts for numerous articles
and hurts when her child is hurt

a mother is a person
who needs to remember
she is a person

MARY ELEANORE RICE

In the midst of all life's daily demands, I AM.

Ministering to Human Need

We need women ministers – ordained and unordained. Women can help because the cultural scripts we carry have constantly put us in a place of weakness. We know our way round this place and, while it is painful for us, it is not somewhere we fear. Biblical and theological scripts have put us, with Eve, in a place of sin. In the new language women are learning in today's Church we have discovered that we are not guilty of this sin. Our mistake has been to believe the messages that made us feel guilty. In this we misnamed our sin. The irony is that we are ideally placed to help everyone learn that we need to be afraid neither of weakness nor of sin, only of our vain attempts to avoid either. Women are throwing off the mantle of guilt and learning the song of freedom.

LAVINIA BYRNE

Suffering for Christ

Men called her Lollard, and women came running out of their houses with their distaffs, crying to the people. 'Burn this false heretic' . . . (They) said to her, 'Woman, give up this life you lead, and go and spin, and card wool, as other women do, and do not suffer so much shame and so much unhappiness. We would not suffer so much for any money on earth.'

Then she said to them, 'I do not suffer as much sorrow as I would do for our Lord's love, for I only suffer cutting words, and our merciful Lord Jesus Christ – worshipped be his name – suffered hard strokes, bitter scourgings, and shameful death at the last, for me and for all mankind, blessed may he be.'

The said creature, lying in her bed on the following night, heard with her bodily ears a loud voice calling, 'Margery.' With that voice she awoke, greatly frightened and, lying still in silence, she said her prayers as devoutly as she could at the time. And soon our merciful Lord, everywhere present, comforting his unworthy servant, said to her, 'Daughter, it is more pleasing to me that you suffer scorn and humiliation, shame and rebukes, wrongs and distress, than if your head were struck off three times a day every day for seven years. And therefore, daughter, do not fear what any man can say to you. But in my goodness, and in your sorrows that you have suffered, you have great cause to rejoice, for when you come home to heaven, then shall every sorrow be turned to joy for you.'

MARGERY KEMPE (B. CIRCA 1373)

God's Grace

To struggle
Laugh and smile
In the midst of aggression;
To be cheerful
To hope, to love
And not to be intimidated,
This is the Grace of God.

NICARAGUA

The Drama of St George

I am St George:
I gallop about on my white horse doing deeds.
I have just found my princess.
I am killing the dragon.
I do not yet know that
The dragon has already submitted.

I am the dragon:
Without me there would be no drama.
I kill people and I eat little girls.
Everyone must die sometime.
I know my time has come.
I submit, willingly.

I am the Princess:
I live in a castle with my family.
I am safe inside.
Now it is time for me to come out.
I stand at the door holding the thread of my destiny.
I can see my Prince killing the dragon.
I do not yet know that
I have already tamed the dragon.
The other end of the thread is round its throat.

I am God:
I am veiled in an arc of the heavenly sphere.
Only I know
The whole story.

I am the girls eaten by the dragon:
Some have been digested into dragon substance.
Some still sing, shout and struggle in its stomach.
Some have become little birds, free to come and go through the jaws.

HEBE WELBOURNE

Come Out of the Kitchen, Martha

Come out of the kitchen, Martha
Listen.

But Lord, much needs attention
And there are no hands but mine.

Come out of the kitchen, Martha
Look.

I will Lord, only let me finish
It is all for you
I see your needs Lord
And am busy.

Come out of the kitchen Martha
Sit.

I cannot sit Lord
My work is here
Women should serve
I know my place Lord
And I am content.
Mary, who lingers at your feet,
I love.
'Tho I must work alone
Forgoing all her help
To leave her listening.
Lord we all have our station
It seems it's hers to sit
And mine to serve . . .

Lord, are you thirsty now?
Or hungry?
I will meet your need
If it is food
I'll hurry now and bring it through.

Come out of the kitchen, Martha
Learn!

Come out of the kitchen Martha
I have need
Of you!

SUSAN ALDRIDGE

Mary and Martha

In the story of the meal at Martha and Mary's house Jesus challenged man's idea of woman as a functional object, a pair of hands to wait on him and be solely concerned with domestic affairs. He did not pat Martha on the back for being a good housewife or exhort Mary to fulfil the traditional role of women. Instead he showed that even the most perfect of men needed women's fellowship, not to dominate or possess, but in the joy and awareness of each other's inner being. Mary is described as 'sitting at the Lord's feet' hearing his word, a phrase used in all religious traditions to denote true discipleship, and Luke's statement that Mary sat at the feet of Jesus may well be an acknowledgement that she was counted as a full disciple, in the same sense as were Peter, James and John. If this was so, then Jesus is saying that he will not allow the discipleship of women to be taken from them.

PHOEBE WILLETTS (1917–1978)

Risktaking

Collect for Pentecost

Spirit of truth
whom the world can never grasp,
touch our hearts
with the shock of your coming;
fill us with desire
for your disturbing peace;
and fire us with longing
to speak your uncontainable word
through Jesus Christ, Amen.

JANET MORLEY

I Am Trusting Thee, Lord Jesus

I am trusting Thee, Lord Jesus,
   Trusting only Thee;
Trusting Thee for full salvation,
    Great and free.

I am trusting Thee for pardon,
   At Thy feet I bow;
For Thy grace and tender mercy
    Trusting now.

I am trusting Thee for cleansing
   In the crimson flood;
Trusting Thee to make me holy
    By Thy blood.

I am trusting Thee to guide me;
   Thou alone shalt lead,
Every day and hour supplying
    All my need.

I am trusting Thee for power,
   Thine can never fail;
Words which Thou Thyself shalt give me
    Must prevail.

I am trusting Thee, Lord Jesus;
   Never let me fall;
I am trusting Thee for ever,
    And for all.

FRANCES RIDLEY HAVERGAL (1836–79)

Loving for Love's Sake

If thou must love me, let it be for naught
Except for love's sake only. Do not say,
'I love her for her smile . . . her look . . . her way
Of speaking gently, . . . for a trick of thought
That falls in well with mine, and brought
A sense of pleasant ease on such a day' –
For these things in themselves, Beloved, may
Be changed, or change for thee, – and lose so wrought,
May be unwrought so. Neither love me for
Thine own dear pity's wiping my cheeks dry,
A creature might forget to weep, who bore
Thy comfort long, and lose thy love thereby!
But love me for love's sake, that evermore
Thou may'st love on through love's eternity.

ELIZABETH BARRETT BROWNING (1806–61)

Bondage

Must I love again, knowing that love grows cold?
Is my heart to be plundered,
And fresh bonds take the place of the old,
So painfully sundered?
Love is a bondage, a torment, a strife –
All three.
May I love, by God's grace, to the end of my life,
Never free.

JOAN LAMBURN

Proposal

Overnight it's Autumn:
The sun is bright and cold
And a thin mist on the river.
The third trimester of our love
Hatched in Spring,
Fledged in Summer, now
Flexing stronger wings,
Examining maturer plumage.
Poised on the cliff-edge,
Measuring the landscape;
Soon it will be colder,
More serious weather,
Harder going, not plain sailing.
Yet it's a passage freely chosen,
Appropriately pinioned –
See the rocks down there?
The valleys, the unknown crevasses?
I see them. Are you ready?
Shall we fly?

ROWENA EDLIN-WHITE

Affirming the Feminine

As I came to own and accept my own womanhood as a gift from God, bringing my own new value for the female side of life into prayer, I experienced a kind of inward leaping which was ecstatically physical as well as spiritual; an inward bodily leaping that made me feel God in my nerves and blood and deep down in my bone marrow as in my emotions and my intellect.

I was not able to approach God with this kind of engagement until I began to open up my prayer life to the feminine aspects of God, and to celebrate my own femaleness in that aspect. And I didn't suspect the wholeness I missed until I began to experience it . . . Now I know with my whole being that I am connected with God . . . and that the realization of this connection is the reason for which I was born.

ALLA BOZARTH-CAMPBELL

May the Wine of the Divine Feminine

May the wine of the Divine Feminine
be created in you,
as it was in Christ,
as it was in Mary of Magdala.
Her beloved died.
Her desire for him,
and her newly healed self,
descended to ferment.

May the wine of the Divine Feminine
flow through you,
as it flowed through Christ,
as it flowed through Mary of Magdala.
She knew him still,
in her own separateness,
and from her depths
new wine rose.

May the wine of the Divine Feminine
send you forth,
as it helped send Mary of Magdala.
They touched for a moment –
companion lovers –
and she is free to tell
'Love is risen.'

MARY ROBINS

Mary Magdalene

Mary Magdalene is not meek and submissive, as good Christian women are often expected to be. The gospel pictures set her apart from all devout virgins and widows, nuns and sisters of famous saints who founded religious nursing orders, the sort of women who are held up to generations of schoolgirls as models of devotion.

In contrast, Mary comes across as a flesh and blood human being whose acts of devotion were extravagant and sincere. Driven by a deep search for love and her own wholeness, she found herself at odds with the male disciples whose concerns often centred around power and personal greatness. Yet when Simon the Pharisee criticized her, Jesus took her side, and held her up as someone who understood the meaning of salvation, in sharp contrast to many religious people of the day: 'Much has been forgiven her, for she has loved much.'

KATHY KEAY

Anna: a Meditation for Candlemas

One day in your courts
Is better than a thousand elsewhere,
And I have spent my thousands in this place
My wealth coined in love stretched out
Through days of waiting
Into your toothless anciency.
Sure of Your advent;
Willing to risk a prophecy
I have spent my barren days before You
Looking for a new light since mine was extinguished
After seven short years
For fresh water, to bring the fecund truth of words fulfilled
The fruitfulness of dry days thirst relieved.

And perhaps You are here;
Dare I risk the final recognition
Final ridicule with this doddering, venerable companion
Who seems so sure You'll set them all alight.
My skin is parchment, and my eyes no longer see
Those visions of my youth
Once clear, before the croaking voice of doubt
Of cold age's experience spoken.

There are no certainties
But still the city groans for God
Crying, 'Who will save us?'
And all these dry days I have awaited You
And now perhaps You have come.

FLORA WINFIELD

Long Barren

Thou who didst hang upon a barren tree,
My God, for me;
  Tho' till now be barren, now at length,
  Lord, give me strength
To bring forth fruit to Thee.

Thou who didst bear for me the crown of thorn,
Spitting and scorn,
  Tho' I till now have put forth thorns, yet now
  Strengthen me Thou
That better fruit be borne.

Thou Rose of Sharon, Cedar of broad roots,
Vine of sweet fruits,
  Thou Lily of the vale with fadeless leaf,
  Of thousands Chief,
Feed Thou my feeble shoots.

CHRISTINA ROSSETTI (1830–94)

Abandonment

Abandonment is not just hanging loose.
It is letting go.
It is a severing of the strings by which one
manipulates
controls
administrates
the forces of one's life.
Abandonment is receiving things the way one receives
a gift
with opened hands
and opened heart.
Abandonment to God
Is the climactic point in anyone's life.

SHEILA CASSIDY

Abandonment is receiving all things the way one receives a gift. Abandonment to God is an act which involves the willingness to receive.

Trust

Remember always that there are two things more easily incompatible than oil and water – trust and worry. Would you call it trust if you should give something into the hands of a friend to attend to for you, and then should spend your nights and days in anxious thought and worry as to whether it should be rightly and successfully done? If you have trusted God in a few things, and He has not failed you, trust Him now for everything, and see if He does not do for you exceeding abundantly, above all that you could ever have asked or even thought.

HANNAH WHITALL SMITH (1832–1911)

Trust is an increasingly confident act of relinquishment into the hands of One you can rely on completely.

Climbing

A Journey Prayer

God, bless to me this day,
God, bless to me this night;
Bless, O bless, Thou God of grace,
Each day and hour of my life;
   Bless, O bless, Thou God of grace,
   Each day and hour of my life.

God, bless the pathway on which I go,
God, bless the earth that is beneath my sole;
Bless, O God, and give to me Thy love.
O God of gods, bless my rest and my repose;
   Bless, O God, and give to me Thy love,
   And bless, O God of gods, my repose.

CARMINA GADELICA

Prayer

Stop walking.
Listen.
Silence?
A drip of water,
A falling leaf,
A robin's trill, seductive, peaceful,
The distant swearing of
A frightened wren.
And behind all these, the highway
Where engines rattle and hum,
And bay like wolves on
The urgent journey to work or pleasure,
Or death.
Laid-by, my closed eyes screen
The spinning motion of a traffic stream.
Eyes, opening, focus on a bright patch:
A glass-bright puddle reflects
White sky and autumn branches.
My soul dives through the white hole
To silence . . .
And surfaces in a flurry of crystal drops
Like a bird, bathed and ready
For the journey.

HEBE WELBOURNE

Up-hill

Does the road wind up-hill all the way?
   Yes, to the very end.
Will the day's journey take the whole long day?
   From morn to night, my friend.

But is there for the night a resting-place?
   A roof for when the slow dark hours begin?
May not the darkness hide it from my face?
   You cannot miss that inn.

Shall I meet other wayfarers at night?
   Those who have gone before.
Then must I knock, or call when just in sight?
   They will not keep you standing at that door.

Shall I find comfort, travel-sore and weak?
   Of labour you shall find the sum.
Will there be beds for me and all who seek?
   Yea, beds for all who come.

CHRISTINA ROSSETTI (1830–94)

'I am the Way'

Thou art the Way.
Hadst Thou been nothing but the goal,
I cannot say
If Thou hadst ever met my soul.

I cannot see –
I, a child of process – if there lies
An end for me,
Full of repose, full of replies.

I'll not reproach
The road that winds, my feet that err.
Access, Approach
Art Thou, Time, Way, and Wayfarer.

ALICE MEYNELL (1847–1923)

Beckoning Grace

We Peters
Walking on Life's sea
Implore
Beckoning grace
In the face
Of heaving waves
Oh let us be
Dear God
However weak
Intent to lean
On Thee.

KATHY KEAY

Simplicity

How happy is the little stone
That rambles in the road alone,
And doesn't care about careers,
And exigencies never fears;
Whose coat of elemental brown
A passing universe put on;
And independent as the sun,
Associates or glows alone,
Fulfilling absolute decree
In casual simplicity.

EMILY DICKINSON (1830–86)

The Faith of a Child

In the old days there were angels who came and took men by the hand
and led them away from the city of destruction. We see no white-
winged angels now. But yet men are led away from a threatening
destruction; a hand is put into theirs, which leads them forth gently
towards a calm and bright land, so that they look no more backward;
and the hand may be a little child's.

FROM *SILAS MARNER*
GEORGE ELIOT (1819–80)

The Edge

Three times to the world's end I went,
Three times returned as one who brings
Tidings of light beyond the dark
But voiceless stays, still marvelling.

After great pain I had great joy
Three times that never else I knew;
The last reflection of its light
Fades from the pupils of my eyes.

Webbed by the world again I walk
The mazy paths that women tread
Watchful lest any harm should come
To those who journeyed back with me.

But still, as Lazarus who was born
Again beyond the edge of death,
I see the world half otherwise
And tremble at its mysteries.

ROSEMARY DOBSON

Jesus, Our Mother

A kind, loving mother who understands and knows the needs of her
child will look after it tenderly just because it is the nature of a mother
to do so. As the child grows older she changes her methods – but not
her love. Older still, she allows the child to be punished so that its
faults are corrected and its virtues and graces developed. This way of
doing things, with much else that is right and good, is our Lord at
work in those who are doing them. Thus he is our Mother in nature,
working by his grace in our lower part, for the sake of the higher. It is
his will that we should know this, for he wants all our love to be
fastened on himself. Like this I could see that our indebtedness, under
God, to fatherhood and motherhood – whether it be human or divine –
is fully met in truly loving God.

JULIAN OF NORWICH (1342–1443)

God Draws Me

he holds his pencil in his hand
but the pencil grows out of his hand
bare branch out of a trunk
sapling out of the ground

and the lead is blended of old ash
from the death of refiner's fires
and burnt trees weighted to the earth's core
and ancient black corroding nails
fallen into dust

and as the point touches the white paper
a line unfurls like a leaf
and another
and it is my curved side
and inclining limbs

and I move dark and live as flame
under his finger

and pray

VERONICA ZUNDEL

A Kind of Prayer

You must learn a kind of prayer that may be exercised at all times, a kind that does not obstruct outward employments, and may be practised equally by princes, kings, prelates, priests and magistrates, soldiers and children, tradesmen, labourers, women, and sick persons. It is the prayer not of the head but of the heart. It is not a prayer of the understanding alone, but the prayer of the heart. Nothing can interrupt this prayer but discarded affections; and when once we have enjoyed God and the sweetness of his love, we shall find it impossible to relish anything but himself.

JEANNE GUYON (1648–1717)

Jesus Taught Us to Pray

God, beloved parent, hear us,
Father and Mother both,
In perfect symmetry;
Far beyond and yet within us –
Excellent mystery!
Holy, Holy, Holy One,
We praise you in your glory.
May your kingdom
Which mysteriously abides
In the Now and the Not Yet
Be manifest among us.
May your first intentions
For your good creation
And your imaged creatures
Be finally fulfilled
Without hindrance of our making.
Feed us, El Shaddai, Sustainer,
That daily we may live and flourish,
Each according to our needs –
And not just bread, O Lord, but roses!
Bread for the body; beauty for the spirit.
Have mercy on us for our failings
And make us merciful when others fail us,
Not niggardly, but in abundance.
Give us strength to turn away from evil,
Wisdom to avoid the snares of the Accuser.
And in the day of trial, protect your children.

Because you alone can do this,
You alone are holy,
Everything is yours, made by you,
Yesterday, today, forever,
From everlasting to everlasting.
Amen, Amen.

ROWENA EDLIN-WHITE

Standing Together

Benediction

The blessing of the God of Sarah, Hagar and
   Abraham,
The blessing of the Son, born of Mary
and the blessing of the Holy Spirit of love
who broods over us as a mother over her children,
be with us all.
Amen.

ECUMENICAL WORKSHOP FOR WOMEN THEOLOGICAL EDUCATORS,
BOSSEY, SWITZERLAND 1991

The Lost Coin

The whole creation is beloved by God. Like the woman who swept and cleaned her house in search of a lost coin, we affirm that God cares for even the last detail of this, God's household, into which we are placed. Women who care for life and nurture it in the daily events of their lives have always been part of that loving relationship towards all that is and the whole of creation.

WOMEN'S STATEMENT TO CONFERENCE OF JUSTICE, PEACE AND THE INTEGRITY OF CREATION

It Takes Two to Share a Vision

What then of Mrs Moses? For if Moses was the focal point of Israel's self-consciousness as the people of God, his wife can be used not only to symbolize the women of Israel but also the search of all women for their own Vision of God. Moses, by going alone to the top of the mountain, could not see the feminine face of God. Women can no longer accept man's description as the sole evidence of the Vision of God's glory, but had Mrs Moses climbed the mountain herself she too would have seen half of God's glory. Only when the Vision of God is shared will we have a fully dimensional view.

We must open our eyes and see that the New Torah in Christ includes women's Vision of God as well as man's. Moses and the prophets only had flickering glimpses of the Vision, but for us it is seen in a person, the Person of Jesus the Christ.

PHOEBE WILLETTS (1917–1978)

Priesthood

if God having body was once and away
and never assumed is never redeemed
then God's body is always male and unbleeding
and mine unredeemed, unredeemable

but here am I woman at the crossway
this is my body
and here am I swallowing bread and red wine
which turns to my body
and here are we sisters, brothers, flame on our brows
we are his body

then God has a female body now
body which bleeds
makes wine into blood
bleeds into life

VERONICA ZUNDEL

A Certain Priest, Observed

How does your black waistcoat
Button me out of the church?
Each button to be unfastened
Before I can creep in
through a button-hole
And hide in your handkerchief pocket.

You fear me, and fasten yourself
neatly, tightly, up to the neck
So that I will not be your undoing.

But I do not want you to give me
your beautiful black buttons
your black waistcoat that secures and binds.

I will wear my green witches' scarf
corn-gold and pink
and loosely knotted
I do not fear being undone
Because God has untied all myself
so that I could dance up to the altar
And lift the cup
And sing.

Perhaps, when I can do this, you
will yourself undo
All those little black buttons.

FLORA WINFIELD

It Was a Woman

It was a woman
who watched over her little brother
when he was hidden in the bulrushes.

It was a woman
who urged her father to perform his vow,
although her own life might be sacrificed.

It was a woman
who so beautifully said 'All was well'
when she came to implore the prophet to restore
her dead and only son.

It was a woman
who followed her mother-in-law
in all her distress and poverty.

It was a woman
who offered her last mite to charity.

It was a woman
who washed our blessed Saviour's feet with her tears
and afterwards wiped them with her hair.

It was a woman
who said, 'Lord if you hadst been here,
my brother had not died!'

It was a woman
who stood at the foot of the Cross.

It was a woman
who went first to the sepulchre.

It was to a woman
our Lord first made himself known
after his resurrection.

MOTHER'S UNION, TASMANIA

Lady in Waiting

Waiting – for what?
For your child to wake,
To need you, to leave you?
For the coming of Christ?
For social security, justice, aid?
For a lucky chance?
For the passage of time?
Enduring the pain
Which can only be borne
Enfolded in the space
Between times.
Lady, let me join you
In the space between,
Where all joys and sorrows are
Meeting.

HEBE WELBOURNE

Folding the Sheets

You and I will fold the sheets
Advancing towards each other
From Burma, from Lapland,

From India where the sheets have been washed in the river
And pounded upon stones:
Together we will match the corners.

From China where women on either side of the river
Have washed their pale cloth in the White Stone Shallows
'Under the shining moon'.

We meet as though in the formal steps of a dance
To fold the sheets together, put them to air
In wind, in sun over bushes, or by the fire.

We stretch and pull from one side and then the other –
Your turn. Now mine.
We fold them and put them away until they are needed.

A wish for all people when they lie down to sleep –
Smooth linen, cool cotton, the fragrance and stir of herbs
And the faint but perceptible scent of sweet clear water.

ROSEMARY DOBSON

Meditation on Friendship

Sometimes one meets a kindred soul,
Stretching out the hand of friendship
To grief, itself a deep dark hole
The hand extends a strong firm grip

To hold, to climb into the light,
Towards the sun, the world and life
Away from fear, dismay and night
To leave behind the pain, the strife

The friendly smile, the listening ear,
Consolation in my time of need,
Kindness, to wipe away each tear,
The hand of friendship, strength indeed

Into the depths there came a hand,
Helping me through the nightmare time
To face the world, to make a stand
By friendship's sake, I made that climb

MARGARET ROOS

Friendship

Oh the comfort, the inexpressible comfort of feeling safe with a person;
having neither to weigh thoughts not measure words, but to pour them all
out, just as they are, chaff and grain together, knowing that a faithful hand
will take and sift them, keep what is worth keeping, and then, with the
breath of kindness, blow the rest away.   GEORGE ELIOT (1819–1880)

Pembrokeshire Coast Path August 1989

There were companions present along the path:
Fulmars, kittiwakes, and a school of porpoises and
A wistful solitary seal.
Stone age man (and woman), corporate,
Having their stone pillars like
A line of ants.
Saints David, Govan, Sampson and Non
Weaving a presence of prayer from the surf
And drifting mist.
And us, two women in present time
On a common path,
Sharing companionship and generating
A new presence.

HEBE WELBOURNE

Leaving Early

We were all there,
Each one of us —
At the party.

We were all there, laughing
With our coats off.

We saw the mother
Dancing,
And the gardener
With patches of purple and pink in her hand.
And we saw the friend
Appear to welcome
And bring them in.

We saw the writer,
Writing,
And the teacher with
A thousand lessons to give,
And when the drinks
Came round
She became the pupil
And carried our bags.

We saw the thinker,
Thinking –
At the party,
And the talker,
Talk,
And we saw her running
When she could but walk.

We saw the giver,
Give,
And the lover,
Love.
We saw the tears and the pain
When enough was enough.

We were all there,
At the party,
Still with our coats off
When someone turned off the music.

And had to leave early.

LUCY DAVIS

The Weavers

We have co-operated in this work,
In this creation.
Although we had no clear idea
Of what it would become,
No vision of its design, at the start.
Still, we threaded the loom
In risk,
Allowing one another to see
Our colours and patterns emerge
As we wove the strands together.
Common patterns
Shared and recognized and given honour,
Creating together a seamless garment of story,
Woven in one piece, from top to bottom.
An infinitely beautiful and varied cloak
Coloured with the clear and shining shades
Of our experience.
And we have used it to dress
The naked imperfections
Of our relationships,
And have been bound together
In the necessary sharing of this creation.

But soon, a time will come
When we must cut this garment from the loom.
Perhaps it will disintegrate
Its manufacture being too random
And too disparate.
Or, perhaps, it will come into its own
Seen and appreciated
As for the first time
Away from the loom's difficult, supporting structure.

Or, will we reach down
And tear our work
And destroy it
Because we cannot bear to share and have shared
In its creation?
Let us leave ourselves at least
A decent covering
For our nakedness.

FLORA WINFIELD

Struggle

Who Shall Deliver Me?

God strengthen me to bear myself;
That heaviest weight of all to bear,
Inalienable weight of care.

All others are outside myself;
I lock the door and bar them out,
The turmoil, tedium, gad-about.

I lock the door upon myself,
And bar them out; but who shall wall
Self from myself; most loathed of all?

If I could once lay down myself,
And start self-purged upon the race
That all must run! Death runs apace.

If I could set aside myself,
And start with lightened heart upon
The road by all men undergone!

God harden me against myself,
This coward with pathetic voice
Who craves for ease, and rest, and joys:

Myself, arch-traitor to myself;
My hollowest friend, my deadliest foe,
My clog whatever road I go.

Yet one there is can curb myself,
Can roll the strangling load from me,
Break off the yoke and set me free.

CHRISTINA ROSSETTI (1830–94)

Pain and Passion

I've got a pain
And passion
In my breast
Which has fired me
Through the best
Part of my life
When they take it
From me
As they must
There will still be pain
And passion
Dispersed
Deeper
And inoperable.

KATHY KEAY

Protest

I do not ask why
Because I have learnt
That Life
And Death come to us
Often suddenly
Arbitrarily.
Yet after 22 years
Of pilgrimage
My God
Still I protest
At the thought of
Radical surgery
And the surgeon's knife
Taking from me
My right breast.

KATHY KEAY

Grant Us Peace

Grant us peace, Lord
as with you we face our trial.
For strength to call our own
we do not ask,
since all we have,
and all that we must have,
is yours for us.
Help us to see
in every action done for us,
your hand;
in every prayer and voice, your word;
for you are here to care for us.
Yet when we cannot see or feel or hear
you close at hand,
you look and touch and listen
and support us more than ever.
You grant us peace, Lord,
that we cannot grasp,
for you sustain with gentle grip;
and only what is strong
can be so imperceptible.
Thank God.

CHRISTINE AND DAVID HARDING

Lord of the Winds

Lord of the winds, I cry to Thee,
  I that am dust,
And blown about by every gust
  I fly to Thee.

Lord of the waters, unto Thee I call.
  I that am weed upon the waters borne,
And by the waters torn,
    Tossed by the waters, at Thy feet I fall.

MARY COLERIDGE (1861–1907)

I Will Live and Survive

I will live and survive and be asked:
How they slammed my head against a trestle,
How I had to freeze at nights,
How my hair started to turn grey . . .
But I'll smile. And will crack some joke
And brush away the encroaching shadow.
And I will render homage to the dry September
That became my second birth.
And I'll be asked: 'Doesn't it hurt you to remember?'
Not being deceived by my outward flippancy.
But the former names will detonate my memory –
Magnificent as old cannon.
And I will tell of the best people in all the earth,

The most tender, but also the most invincible,
How they said farewell, how they went to be tortured,
How they waited for letters from their loved ones.
And I'll be asked: what helped us to live
When there were neither letters nor any news – only walls
And the cold of the cell, and the blather of official lies,
And the sickening promises made in exchange for betrayal.
And I will tell of the first beauty
I saw in captivity.
A frost-covered window! No spyholes, nor walls,
Nor cell-bars, nor the long-endured pain –
Only a blue radiance on a tiny pane of glass,
A cast pattern – none more beautiful could be dreamt!
The more clearly you looked, the more powerfully blossomed
Those brigand forests, campfires and birds!
And how many times, there was bitter cold weather
And how many windows sparkled after that one –
But it was never repeated,
That upheaval of rainbow ice!
And anyway, what good would it be to me now,
And what would be the pretext for that festival?
Such a gift can only be received once,
And perhaps is only needed once.

IRINA RATUSHINSKAYA

Song for Kathy

Some say that death comes in his hour
the crown and crest of life
and some say death's a demon power
and some say death's a knife

but I say death's a hasty child
that will not wait for time
but snatches young and bright and wild
and beauty in her prime

and death's a vandal, death's a knave
that smashes down the door
and none but only one can save
my darlings from his claw

VERONICA ZUNDEL

Losing

We laugh and call to one another –
'Thanks for coming in – goodbye!'
We struggle with our losses, you and I.
You the dead, the Christmas suicide,
Me the rubbing out of something newer.
Oh God! You waited with us for the verdict,
Put your arms around us as we took it in,
Hold us now, so gently, in your love
Through the lonely evenings and cold nights,
The bleak mornings, empty afternoons;
Compensate us for the absent human arms and loving,
Listen as we talk aloud to air
And, in the sobbing twilight, touch our hair.

Father, you give your daughters strength,
A double portion to sustain us through
The loneliness of loss and leaving,
The child, the man, forced from our breast.
Help us to turn and trust you for the rest.

ROWENA EDLIN-WHITE

O Holy Water

O holy water
Love, I learn
I may not take thee
Though I burn.

O frustrate passion
Supple vine,
I tear thy tendrils
Waste thy wine.

O jagged path
Reality
I weep and bleed
To follow thee.

MARGOT RUDDOCK (1907–51)

Good Friday in My Heart

Good Friday in my heart! Fear and affright!
My thoughts are the Disciples when they fled,
My words the words that priest and soldier said,
My deed the spear to desecrate the dead.
And day, Thy death therein, is changed to night.

Then Easter in my heart sends up the sun.
My thoughts are Mary, when she turned to see.
My words are Peter, answering, 'Lov'st thou Me?'
My deeds are all Thine own drawn close to Thee,
And night and day, since Thou dost rise, are one.

MARY COLERIDGE (1861–1907)

Crucifixus Est

I bring you
my anger and my pain
and beneath your feet
I nail them to the tree
with splinters of my hope

forgive me, for I have sinned
love me, for I have nothing else.

LIZ KNOWLES

Faith

And is the great cause lost beyond recall?
Have all the hopes of ages come to naught?
Is life no more with noble meaning fraught?
Is life but death, and love its funeral pall?
Maybe. And still on bended knees I fall,
Filled with a faith no preacher ever taught.
O God – *my* God – by no false prophet wrought –
I believe still, in despite of it all!

Let go the myths and creeds of groping men.
This clay knows naught – the Potter understands.
I own that Power divine beyond my ken.
And still can leave me in His shaping hands.
But, O my God, that madest me to feel,
Forgive the anguish of the turning wheel!

ADA CAMBRIDGE (1844–1926)

Be With Me, O God

Be with me, O God, in time of deep adversity, which is apt to affect my mind too much and to dispose to anxious, doubtful and unbelieving thoughts. May I give way to no direct murmurings, no repinings at the prosperity of others, no harsh reflections on Providence, but may I maintain a constant acknowledgement of Thy justice and goodness. Save me from thinking severely or unjustly of others: from being too much dejected or disposed to peevishness, covertousness, or negligence in affairs: from working too much or too little. Forbid that I should ever wholly omit to implore Thy divine blessing and assistance in honest prospects and endeavours, or be too solicitous and earnest in prayer for external blessings. May no slight access of trouble have power to ruffle my temper, and to indispose or distract my mind in my addresses to Heaven, in reading, meditation or any other spiritual exercise. I would ever lay to heart the words of our Lord: 'Be careful (anxious) for nothing. Therefore I say unto you, Be not anxious for the morrow.' Amen.

SUSANNA WESLEY (1669–1742)

In Heavenly Love Abiding

In heavenly love abiding,
  No change my heart shall fear;
And safe is such confiding,
  For nothing changes here:
The storm may roar without me,
  My heart may low be laid;
But God is round about me,
  And can I be dismayed?

Wherever He may guide me,
  No want shall turn me back;
My Shepherd is beside me,
  And nothing can I lack:
His wisdom ever waketh,
  His sight is never dim;
He knows the way He taketh,
  And I will walk with Him.

Green pastures are before me,
  Which yet I have not seen;
Bright skies will soon be o'er me,
  Where the dark clouds have been:
My hope I cannot measure,
  My path to life is free;
My Saviour has my treasure,
  And He will walk with me.

ANNA LAETITIA WARING (1820–1910)

Peace

I will reach into
the still small point
which is
at the centre
of my soul
and whisper
PEACE
PEACE
until
all the clamour
of vain worlds
cease
and I emerge
more whole.

Kathy Keay

Wilderness

Collect for Lent 1

Spirit of Integrity,
you drive us into the desert
to search out our truth.
Give us clarity to know what is right,
and courage to reject what is strategic;
that we may abandon the false innocence
of failing to choose at all,
but may follow the purposes of Jesus Christ,
Amen.

JANET MORLEY

Hope Deferred

Why, lovely swallow, weary me with thy sweet chattering?
What dost thou hope to find in my heart? The warmth of the Spring?
In the great azure are flaming the almond bough and the almandine
   flower of the clear rose,
And my heart sheds its fire.

For once it was Spring. But now there is neither honey nor bee for me –
Neither the sting nor the sweetness.
Not mine the warm heart of Aprils and apricots, apricus.
Sunny, all gold within like the heart of the honeycomb,
Neither the honey-winged swarms of the golden thoughts of summer
Shall be mine again!

EDITH SITWELL (1887–1964)

*Although everything within me may deny outward signs of Spring, the soul has
its seasons, and surely as the buds appear, new life WILL come to me also, so I
shall NOT despair.*

She Climbed a Mountain

She climbed a mountain
That year,
Many a time she found
Her foot slipping
On the shale,
Setting a cascade hurtling
To the ground.

She wondered
How she reached the top.
Driving herself on
She reckoned it would be worth
It when she stopped.
But the summit
Was in cloud
And even though she felt proud
At succeeding
She never managed to come down to earth.

Someone said to her once
To stop fighting.
For fighting the feeling caused the pain.
But she never managed
To get off that mountain
Or destroy the feeling
Hoping one day
He'd be there,
Hoping one day

Her mind would stop reeling
And she'd see Him.
There seemed no point now
To her climb
As she lingered on the ledge.
The nothingness below
Fuelled her fear
And she waited to be pushed
Over the edge.

LUCY DAVIS

Disillusionment

It is hard
living at the level
where all dreams are shattered
where no secrets are hid
and where all desires are known
and exposed.
It is hard
painfully hard
like walking on broken glass
where once there was sand
with no one to hold your hand now.

I pace my way across
the splintered surface
cutting deeper into wounds
already made
and see from side to side
images of children
playing freely
laughing and jostling
before me
and I wonder what their fate will be
as I watch from my path
for I see that they
like me
have walked on sand.

KATHY KEAY

Tragedy

Lord, let not the darkness
In my heart
Prevent me from showing others
The full dynamic
Of your redeeming love.
Expose and heal
The loneliness from past days.
My pilgrim heart is restless,
Afflicted,
Often pathetically tempted
Away from Thee.

With my consent
Darkness broods,
Time passes
And people –
The potentially all-glorious
Now hurting
Slip unloved
Eternally
Away from Thee

KATHY KEAY

Construction

From the mind's rafters
Out of the heart's rust
I built a city that shone a day
And crumbled into dust.

Then stood I on the scaffolding
Of my own despair,
Trembling lest I should lose hold
So frail my balance there.

O lovely unconstructed tree
O tree stretching to God
Would I could grow alike to thee
And draw from earth my food;
Earth tend for me, earth care for me
That I grow mellow, wrought
Without desire, without despair
And with no thought of thought.

MARGOT RUDDOCK (1907–51)

A Better Resurrection

I have no wit, no words, no tears;
  My heart within me like a stone
Is numbed too much for hopes or fears.
  Look right, look left, I dwell alone;
I lift mine eyes, but dimmed with grief
  No everlasting hills I see;
My life is in the falling leaf:
  O Jesus, quicken me.

My life is like a faded leaf,
  My harvest dwindled to a husk:
Truly my life is void and brief
  And tedious in the barren dusk;
My life is like a frozen thing,
  No bud nor greenness can I see;
Yet rise it shall – the sap of Spring;
  O Jesus, rise in me.

My life is like a broken bowl,
  A broken bowl that cannot hold
One drop of water for my soul
  Or cordial in the searching cold;
Cast in the fire the perished thing;
  Melt and remould it, till it be
A royal cup for Him, my King:
  O Jesus, drink of me.

CHRISTINA ROSSETTI (1830–94)

Naming the Dark Within

Earlier this year I had a revelation on a London bus. The number 12
takes an hour to go from Oxford Circus to the outer darkness of Forest
Hill. I caught it on Regent Street and scrambled up to the last
remaining seat on the top deck, at the back on the right hand side.
After a while I heard a voice calling out, 'Madam, madam.' I turned
round and saw behind me on the left a woman in her twenties. Her
face was puffy and bruised; her bottom teeth had been knocked out;
she was drinking from a can of beer and was asking me for a light . . . I
looked at her with total recognition, with a degree of identification that
would have astonished her fellow travellers. I saw all my own pain and
hurt in her face and in her battered mouth; I heard the polite
institutionalized voice saying, 'Madam, madam,' knowing all the right
words, the mechanics of survival; I saw the outward signs of personal
weakness and need, the beer can, the soggy cigarette. Inside myself I
wept. I wonder what she saw when she looked at me? I wonder if I will
ever understand the extent to which I need to learn the lessons of
darkness that she imaged for me as she asked me for a light.

The following day when cycling down Bond Street I took a slightly
different route from my usual one and found myself drawing up at
some red traffic lights in Mayfair. Then I heard her voice, rasping out
the words, 'News, Evening News'. She was selling newspapers from
her 'pitch'. The odds against our meeting again, our meeting the next
day, within half a mile of where I work, must have been extraordinarily
high. She can come to me for light and I can go to her for news, for
information. And so we can find that each of us lies bleeding at the
other's gate.

LAVINIA BYRNE

With Jacob

inexorably I cry
as I wrestle
for the blessing,
thirsty, straining
for the joining
till my desert throat
runs dry.
I must risk
the shrunken sinew
and the laming of
his naming
till I find
my final quenching
in the hollow
of the thigh.

LUCI SHAW

Message from Home

Do you remember, when you were first a child,
Nothing in the world seemed strange to you?
You perceived, for the first time, shapes already familiar,
And seeing, you knew that you have always known
The lichen on the rock, fern-leaves, the flowers of thyme,
As if the elements newly met in your body,
Caught up into the momentary vortex of your living
Still kept the knowledge of a former state,
In you retained recollection of cloud and ocean,
The branching tree, the dancing flame.

Now when nature's darkness seems strange to you,
And you walk, an alien, in the streets of cities,
Remember earth breathed you into her with the air, with the sun's rays,
Laid you in her waters asleep, to dream
With the brown trout among the milfoil roots,
From substance of star and ocean fashioned you,
At the same source conceived you
As sun and foliage, fish and stream.

Of all created things the source is one,
Simple, single as love . . .

KATHLEEN RAINE

Having a Baby — a Parable of Grace

Having a baby is a unique sort of offering. Virtually no other experience is so rewarding and so demanding at the same time.

Giving birth is a parable of grace, because it is nothing to do with you and everything to do with you.

The first few days after the birth are a mixture of happiness, weariness, frustration and exhilaration, all rolled into one. You seem to spend the whole day (and most of the night) feeding, changing nappies, talking to visitors, doing scraps of housework when there is a moment, and wondering when you will ever be able to relax. One minute you feel bouncy and thankful, and the next you dissolve into tears because you are so worn out and your entire existence seems to have been sucked into caring for the baby. It is a kind of dying for the sake of new life.

How can anyone live contemplatively when faced with the constant needs of a new baby? All patterns of prayer times fly out of the window for the present. We are lucky if we can sit down for the occasional five minutes with a coffee and 'Phew! here I am, Lord!'

The whole incredible mixture of receiving and giving can itself become our prayer. We find ourselves in the middle of a life-giving process which comes from God and is soaked in God. All we need to do is recognize Him there, *in* the broken nights and piles of washing, and in the small person around whom the household revolves at the moment. We may need no more than the words 'Thank you' to express everything.

ANGELA ASHWIN

Once in Regions Void of Light

Once in regions void of light I wandered;
In blank darkness I stumbled,
And fear led me by the hand;
My feet pressed earthward,
Afraid of pitfalls.
By many shapeless terrors of the night affrighted,
To the wakeful day
I held out beseeching arms.

Then came Love, bearing in her hand
The torch that is the light unto my feet,
And softly spoke Love: 'Hast thou
Entered into the treasures of darkness?
Hast thou entered into the treasures of the night?
Search out thy blindness. It holdeth
Riches past computing.'

The words of Love set my spirit aflame.
My eager fingers searched out the mysteries,
The splendours, the inmost sacredness of things,
And in the vacancies discerned
With spiritual sense the fullness of life;
And the gates of Day stood wide.

HELEN KELLER (1880–1968)

Sanctuary

Hiding from the Nazis in Holland during the Second World War, the writer found temporary sanctuary in the attic of a friendly house.

I spent most of my time in true solitary confinement, more mental than physical. My thoughts had always been my own, but here, here it was different; one could not utter these thoughts, mould them, discuss them and get fresh ideas.

Never before did I have such close fellowship with Him the invisible Christ, whose existence people deny. Our acquaintance became strong, our friendship secure, my dependability on Him absolutely unshakeable, a certainty which I have proved in every smallest detail till this very day.

Some of His attitudes have puzzled me. I still don't understand the depth of all His suffering for those who care to associate with Him . . . His promises are dependable and pregnant with fulfilment. With Him one can live through the toughest problems, the most dangerous situation, the loneliest experience. He promised to be with us always, and He is with us in every difficulty. One just cannot doubt Him, when He has proved Himself dependable in every aspect of life.

With warm love He surrounded me in that bare attic. He gave me courage when air raid sirens sounded their fearful piercing tone. When others ran to the shelters, He stayed with me . . . I knew myself loved, even when no human being considered my need. His cross became my symbol of ultimate victory . . . It was the cross which pointed at all times to the Victory after suffering and death.

JOHANNA RUTH DOBSCHINER

God's Faithfulness

But God is not like human-kind;
Man cannot read the Almighty mind;
Vengeance will never torture thee,
Nor hurt thy soul eternally.

Then do not in this night of grief,
This time of overwhelming fear,
O do not think that God can leave,
Forget, forsake, refuse to hear!

EMILY BRONTË (1818–48)

God remains faithful, even when we don't deserve it and fear the worst.

Reflection

Remembering

A thought went up my mind today
That I have had before,
But did not finish, – some way back,
I could not fix the year.

Nor where it went, nor why it came
The second time to me,
Nor definitely what it was,
Have I the art to say.

But somewhere in my soul, I know
I've met the thing before;
It's just reminded me – twas all –
And came my way no more.

EMILY DICKINSON (1830–86)

As You Leave Eden Behind

As you leave Eden behind you, remember your home,
For as you remember back into your own being
You will not be alone; the first to greet you
Will be those children playing by the burn,
The otters will swim up to you in the bay,
The wild deer on the moor will run beside you.

Sleep at the tree's root, where the night is spun
Into the stuff of worlds, listen to the winds,
The tides, and the night's harmonies, and know
All that you knew before you began to forget . . .

KATHLEEN RAINE

The Weak and the Strong

The weakest things in the world can defeat
the strongest things in the world.
Nothing under heaven is more soft and yielding
than water, yet for attacking the solid and
strong nothing is better and nothing its equal.
Weak can overcome strong
Yielding can overcome stiff
Under heaven, all the world knows this.

These are words of truth,
Truth is often spoken in paradox.

TAO TE CHING

Laughter

A sneeze is an explosion,
A little death.
Bless God, says Mother Julian,
Remembering laughter
When the devil departed.
Laughter explodes into resurrection.

HEBE WELBOURNE

A Splash of Colour

O God, save me from being
a dull, grey person,
and let the colours of your creation
pattern my life with your beauty.

KATHY KEAY

On Not Seeing the Kingfisher

I have come daily, in hope,
Yearning for his coming.

The river waits, ripe,
A tunnel of fecundity:
Loosestrife, meadowsweet, comfrey
And their reflections.
In other years he has come —
A flash of blue flame
momentarily transfiguring
The river's vault.

This year I have come daily,
The summer slips by, unfulfilled.
Has he succumbed to
The planet's terminal predator?
Or do I just come
At the wrong time?

And so, now
How do I say, Lord
Now let thy servant depart
In peace?

HEBE WELBOURNE

My God, I Thank Thee

My God, I thank Thee, who has made
   The earth so bright,
So full of splendour and of joy,
   Beauty and light;
So many glorious things are here,
   Noble and right.

I thank Thee, too, that Thou hast made
   Joy to abound,
So many gentle thoughts and deeds
   Circling us around
That in the darkest spot of earth
   Some love is found.

I thank Thee more that all our joy
   Is touched with pain,
That shadows fall on brightest hours,
   That thorns remain,
So that earth's bliss may be our guide,
   And not our chain.

I thank Thee, Lord, that Thou hast kept
   The best in store:
We have enough, yet not too much
   To long for more –
A yearning for a deeper peace
   Not known before.

I thank Thee, Lord, that here our souls,
  Though amply blest,
Can never find, although they seek,
  A perfect rest,
Nor ever shall, until they lean
  On Jesus' breast.

ADELAIDE ANNE PROCTOR (1825–64)

Immanence

I come in the little things,
Saith the Lord:
Not borne on morning wings
Of majesty, but I have set My Feet
Amidst the delicate and bladed wheat
That springs triumphant in the furrowed sod.
There do I dwell, in weakness and in power;
Not broken or divided, saith our God!
In your strait garden plot I come to flower:
About your porch My Vine
Meek, fruitful, doth entwine;
Wait, at the threshold, Love's appointed hour.

I come in the little things,
Saith the Lord:
Yea! on the glancing wings
Of eager birds, the softly pattering feet
Of furred and gentle beasts, I come to meet
Your hard and wayward heart. In brown bright eyes
That peep from out the brake, I stand confest.
On every nest
Where feathery Patience is content to brood
And leaves her pleasure for the high emprise
Of motherhood –
There doth My Godhead rest.

I come in the little things,
Saith the Lord:
My starry wings
I do forsake,
Love's highway of humility to take:
Meekly I fit My stature to your need,
In beggar's part
About your gates I shall not cease to plead –
As man, to speak with man –
Till by such art
I shall achieve My Immemorial Plan,
Pass the low lintel of the human heart.

EVELYN UNDERHILL (1875–1941)

For a Mercy Received

Christina Rossetti wrote a poem called *For a Mercy Received*. I will
endeavour each day I write this journal to record at least one mercy.
To-day it shall be a nicely ironed tray-cloth.

FAY INCHFAWN

Visitations

God is seen
in a baby crying;
in a young man dying
before his time.

God is heard
in the sweet song
of a swallow singing;
in the final note
of a church bell clanging
before the building's closed.

God is felt
in the touch of a young shoot
thriving;
in the body of a loved one
writhing in beauty;
God is present also in striving –
the pain of labour
before new birth;
the thirst of a man
preceding his last breath;
the longing of a father
watching
his son's death
and the joy of a mother
watching the baby
feed from the breast.

O God, our God
how varied are your visitations
amongst us.

KATHY KEAY

A Short and Easy Method of Prayer

The infant hanging at its mother's breast is a lovely illustration. It begins to draw milk, by moving its little lips; but when the milk flows abundantly, it is content to swallow and suspends its suction: by doing otherwise it would hurt itself, spill the milk and be obliged to quit the breast.

We must act in like manner in the beginning of Prayer, by exerting the lips of the affections; but as soon as the milk of Divine Grace flows freely, we have nothing to do, but in repose and stillness, sweetly to imbibe it, and when it ceases to flow, we must again stir up the affections as the infant moves its lips.

JEANNE GUYON (1648–1717)

Listening to God

The most difficult and most decisive part of prayer is acquiring the ability to listen. To listen, according to the dictionary, is 'attentively to exercise the sense of hearing'. It is not a passive affair, a space when we don't happen to be doing or saying anything and are, therefore, automatically able to listen. It is a conscious, willed action, requiring alertness and vigilance, by which our whole attention is focused and controlled. So it is difficult. And it is decisive because it is the beginning of our entry into a personal relationship with God in which we gradually learn to let go of ourselves and allow the Word of God to speak within us.

MOTHER MARY CLARE

Reflection _____ 119

God Speaking

Sometimes I think
it is so slow
not even word by word, but
a diphthong, a vowel, a plosive
painfully pushed out
over hours, days
lips labouring
until at long, long last
the word is formed

and I must listen
slow, so slow
to catch it closing on my ear

and even then, perhaps, mishear

VERONICA ZUNDEL

Comfort

Speak low to me, my Saviour, low and sweet
From out the hallelujahs, sweet and low,
Lest I should fear and fall, and miss Thee so
Who are not missed by any that entreat.
Speak to me as to Mary at Thy feet!
And if no precious gums my hand bestow,
Let my tears drop like amber while I go
In reach of Thy divinest voice complete
In humanist affection – thus, in sooth,
To lose the sense of losing. As a child,
Whose song-bird seeks the wood for evermore,
Is sung to in its stead by mother's mouth
Till, sinking on her breast, love reconciled,
He sleeps the faster that he wept before.

ELIZABETH BARRETT BROWNING (1806–61)

Rising

Hope

Hope is there
like a smouldering fire
that cannot be extinguished . . .
some day that purifying furnace
will heat a decent poor person's stove.

HAITI

God's Hope for the Soul

The true basis of the soul's hope of God is God's hope for the soul. His confident intention precedes and inspires ours, and gives all its significance to our life. God's hope for souls often seems to us to be thwarted; but it begins again in its power and freshness with every baby born into the world. Each represents a hope of God: a possibility of holiness, a fullness of life.   EVELYN UNDERHILL (1875–1941)

The Stone

The future accumulates like a weight upon the past. The weight upon the earliest years is easier to remove to let that time spring up like grass that has been crushed. The years following childhood become welded to their future, massed like stone, and often the time beneath cannot spring back into growth like new grass: it lies bled of its green in a new shape . . . entangled beneath the stone.

FROM An Angel At My Table
Janet Frame

Whatever has been crushed within us over the years, though colourless and buried, will emerge in time, in a new shape, heralding new life and offering new, long awaited possibilities for growth.

Credo

I believe the earth
exists, and
in each minim mote
of its dust the holy
glow of thy candle.
Thou
unknown I know,
thou spirit,
giver,
lover of making, of the

wrought letter,
wrought flower,
iron, deed, dream.
Dust of the earth,
help thou my
unbelief. Drift,
grey becomes gold, in the beam of
vision. I believe and
interrupt my belief with
doubt. I doubt and
interrupt my doubt with belief. Be,
belovèd, threatened world.
                              Each minim
mote.
                    Not the poisonous
luminescence forced
out of privacy,
the sacred lock of its cell
broken. No,
the ordinary glow
of common dust in ancient sunlight
Be, that I may believe. Amen.

FROM *MASS FOR THE DAY OF ST THOMAS DIDYMUS*
                    DENISE LEVERTOV

A Prisoner's Inner Peace

But first a hush of peace, a soundless calm descends;
The struggle of distress and fierce impatience ends;
Mute music soothes my breast — unuttered harmony
That I could never dream till earth was lost to me.

Then dawns the Invisible, the Unseen its truth reveals;
My outward sense is gone, my inward essence feels —
Its wings are almost free, its home, its harbour found;
Measuring the gulf, it stoops and dares the final bound!

EMILY BRONTË (1818–48)

I will not wait 'til I have lost my freedom, I will make the most of what I have NOW.

Choice

Will you continue
To exhaust yourself
Battering your wings
Against immovable bars?
Or will you learn
To live
Within the confines
Of your prison
And find to your surprise
That you have
The strength to sing
Even there?

KATHY KEAY

Courage

A candle is a protest at midnight.
It is a non-conformist.
It says to the darkness,
'I beg to differ'.

INDIAN PROVERB

Do not be afraid of standing up for what you believe; what you do, no matter how small, will make a difference.

Fear Not

Those in power can no longer overlook the handwriting on the wall
their subjects think twice about nodding in agreement
the weapon dealers no longer dare to walk over the weak
bishops stop equivocating and say no
the friends of jesus block the roads of overkill
school children learn the truth.

How are we to recognize an angel
except that he brings courage where fear was
joy where even sadness refused to grow
objections where hard facts used to rule the day
disarmament where terror was a credible deterrent.

Fear not resistance is growing.

DOROTHEE SÖLLE

After Breast Cancer Diagnosis April 1993

Prayer is a silence and a shouting
a burst of praise
a thanksgiving
welling up and out of us
in spite of everything.

*For nothing can separate us from the love of God; nothing in the past or present
or future. Nothing in the heights or depths, in life or in death can separate us
from the love of God shown to us in Christ Jesus our Lord (Romans 8:38-9).*

KATHY KEAY

When a Black Woman Decides to Make a Pot

When a black woman decides to make a pot
The clay is wet and white on her dry hands,

Shaping the soft clay between them
Jeremiah's God's daughter
Remakes the world.

FLORA WINFIELD

The Time for Singing Has Come

The winter is over; the rains have finished;
in the countryside the flowers are blooming.
    This is time for singing;
the cooing of doves is heard in the fields (Song of Songs 2:11, & 12).

*For Christians in China these verses reflect not only the change in seasons, but also
their hope for a better future for all. A popular hymn is based on this text —*

Jesus my Lord, my love, my all,
Body and soul forever yours,
in dale so dark, I long for you,
abide with me in spring anew.

CHINA

Wild Spirit

wild spirit
bird of the brightest hour
of the sun's journey
I have opened your cage
have set you free
wild spirit
let your own self free

wild spirit
your feathered voyage
is to a distant shore
but I have heard
the symphony of your soul
have seen your gilt-edged past
for you have settled there before

wild spirit
bound by fear of flight
I have seen the shiver of thrill
don't mistake it for the tremble of fright
open your own cage
dare to soar peak height
reach the out-of-sight

ELLEN WILKIE (1958–89)

God Is With Us

God is with us, through loneliness, bereavement, broken relationships
and unemployment, as well as at times of great joy and achievement.
Nothing can surprise or shock God. He knows and deeply loves each of
us. Once we understand this we can live life to the full, even against
impossible odds.

KATHY KEAY

Panoramas

Endurance

We women who have lived
through many winters
are sisters to mountain flowers
found in rocky crevices
high in the Alps

Hardened by wind and snow
we endure
cold
absorb brief sun
reach long roots
to meagre sustenance
lift bright blossoms to empty air

FRAN PORTLEY

Via, et Veritas, et Vita

'You never attained to Him?' 'If to attain
Be to abide, then that may be.'
'Endless the way, followed with how much pain!'
   'The way was He.'

ALICE MEYNELL (1847–1923)

All the Prodigals Are Not Sons

All the prodigals are not sons, Father,
She too has wandered,
Daughter of obstinate decisions,
Far from the arms of love:
And as she wandered far and out of sight
Your father love no longer saw,
But waited,
Letting the wanderer go.
Yet still your mother heart
Peeped through the crack of heaven
Into the far and foreign country
Of deliberate rebellion
To keep her wanderings in view.

Perhaps only a daughter could suggest it,
Whose mother heart
Echoes and copies
All the rhythms of your love.
Father of all mankind,
You are yet a mother too to those
Who need a signpost
On the journey.
God of the cross
And of each crossroad,
All the prodigals are not sons, Father,
And the Way grows clearer
As I travel
Home.

SUSAN ALDRIDGE

New Seasons in the Garden

A new season, drive full of snowdrops
Still the challenging frailty
Which incites me: grow, bud, change, risk.
Here in well-known paths I measure
The journey selfwards, soulwards.
Old hurts, grown gnarled, callused over,
Their scars in Mother Julian's terms
Become God's honours, and – see!
Fresh buds greening in risky spring,
Alert to warmth or snowfall.
Paths newly pebbled –
You cannot now
Retread the ways you took once.
Garden, God's microcosm filled
With messages and mystery
Again you tell me:
I have not been here before.

WENDY CAREY

Through the Love of God Our Saviour

Through the love of God our Saviour
   All will be well;
Free and changeless is His favour,
   All, all is well:
Precious is the blood that healed us;
Perfect is the grace that sealed us;
Strong the hand stretched forth to shield us,
   All must be well.

Though we pass through tribulation,
   All will be well;
Christ hath purchased full salvation,
   All, all is well:
Happy still in God confiding;
Fruitful, if in Christ abiding;
Holy, through the Spirit's guiding;
   All must be well.

We expect a bright tomorrow;
   All will be well;
Faith can sing through days of sorrow,
   All, all is well:
On our Father's love relying,
Jesus every need supplying,
Or in living or in dying
   All must be well.

MARY PETERS (1813–56)

All Will be Well

On one occasion the good Lord said, 'Everything is going to be all right.' On another, 'You will see for yourself that every sort of thing will be all right.' In these two sayings the soul discerns various meanings.

One is that he wants us to know that not only does he care for great and noble things, but equally for little and small, lowly and simple things as well. This is his meaning: '*Every*-thing will be all right.' We are to know that the least thing will not be forgotten.

JULIAN OF NORWICH (1342–1443)

It Is Hope's Spell

It is Hope's spell that glorifies
Like youth to my maturer eyes
All Nature's million mysteries –
The fearful and the fair –

Hope soothes me in the griefs I know,
She lulls my pain for others' woe
And makes me strong to undergo
What I am born to bear.

Glad comforter, will I not brave
Unawed the darkness of the grave?
Nay, smile to hear Death's billows rave,
My Guide, sustained by thee?
The more unjust seems present fate
The more my Spirit springs elate
Strong in thy strength, to anticipate
Rewarding Destiny!

EMILY BRONTË (1818-48)

The Passing of the Foremothers

All my dear old friends,
The grandmas of the church,
Limp gamely home.
We waved off Marjorie
On Easter Saturday,
Her little coffin underneath
The banner HE IS RISEN,
And so is she.
And Peggy, Sylvia, Gladys
And the rest,
Foremothers of the faith
Who wiped my nose
When first I came to Jesus;
Steely-haired and golden-hearted
Women twice my age,
Yet sisters, pushing forward
Fearlessly to meet their God
Seen dimly through the dust
At the end of a long road.

ROWENA EDLIN-WHITE

O Ye Who Taste That Love Is Sweet

O ye who taste that love is sweet,
Set waymarks for all doubtful feet
That stumble on in search of it.

Sing notes of love: that some who hear
Far off, inert, may lend an ear,
Rise up and wonder and draw near.

Lead lives of love; that others who
Behold your life may kindle too
With love, and cast their lot with you.

CHRISTINA ROSSETTI (1830–94)

Under a Wiltshire Apple Tree

Some folks as can afford,
So I've heard say,
Set up a sort of cross
Right in the garden way
To mind 'em of the Lord.

But I, when I do see
Thik apple tree
An' stoopin' limb
All spread wi' moss,
I think of Him
And how He talks wi' me.

I think of God
And how He trod
That garden long ago;
He walked, I reckon, to and from
And then sat down
Upon the groun'
Or some low limb
What suited Him
Such as you see
On many a tree,
And on thik very one
Where I at set o' sun
Do sit and talk wi' He.

And, mornings too, I rise and come
An' sit down where the branch be low;
A bird do sing, a bee do hum,
The flowers in the border blow,
And all my heart's so glad and clear
As pools when mists do disappear:
As pools a-laughing in the light
When mornin' air is swep' an' bright,
As pools what got all Heaven in sight
So's my heart's cheer
When He be near.

He never pushed the garden door,
He left no footmark
   on the floor;
I never heard 'Un stir nor tread
And yet His Hand
   do bless my head,
And when 'tis time for work to start
I takes Him with me in my heart.

And when I die, Pray God I see
At very last thik apple tree
An' stoopin' limb,
And think of Him
And all He been to me.

ANNA BUNSTON DE BARY

To My Mother

You are in pain; and it pains me
That you must live your last years out
This way. Whilst I, who will outlive,
Cannot do for you those things you longed to do,
Years of freedom cannot give.

You are afraid; it frightens me
To contemplate the route you take.
The questioning, the 'Can I bear
To go this way?' The route's well plotted. You have
No choice. Choice I cannot give.

You are confused; confusion lies
In wayward amblings of the mind.
The 'Is it right that this should be?'
You ask. I ask, but torn between haste and sloth,
No easy answer can give.

You are a child; and I, full-grown,
Cannot take the child's way through grief,
Discard the years and let trust in.
But you, you are the one of whom Jesus has said
'Let her come and I will give'.

I have no gifts to help you go;
The pain, the fear, confusion too,
Are all the things I can do for you.
But the simple child you can do yourself, and
God knows what gifts to give.

MARGARET MOAKES

Through the Passage Way

I always thought I should love to grow old, and I find it even more
delightful than I thought. It is so delicious to have done with things,
and to feel no need any longer to concern myself much about earthly
affairs. I seem on the verge of a most delightful journey to a place of
unknown joys and pleasures, and things here seem of so little
importance compared to things there . . . The world seems to me
nothing but a passage way to the real life beyond; and passage ways are
very important places . . . I am tremendously content to let one
activity after another go, and to wait quietly and happily the opening of
the door at the end of the passage way, that will let me in to my real
abiding place.

HANNAH WHITALL SMITH (1832–1911)

Resurgam

I shall say, Lord, 'Is it music, is it morning,
Song that is fresh as sunrise, light that sings?'
When on some hill there breaks the immortal warning
Of half-forgotten springs.

I shall say, Lord, 'I have loved you, not another,
Heard in all quiet your footsteps on my road,
Felt your strong shoulder near me, O my brother,
Lightening the load.'

I shall say, Lord, 'I remembered, working, sleeping,
One face I looked for, one denied and dear.
Now that you come my eyes are blind with weeping,
But you will kiss them clear.'

I shall say, Lord, 'Touch my lips, and so unseal them;
I have learned silence since I lived and died.'
I shall say, Lord, 'Lift my hands, and so reveal them
Full, satisfied.'

I shall say, Lord, 'We will laugh again to-morrow,
Now we'll be still a little, friend with friend.
Death was the gate and the long way was sorrow,
Love is the end.

MARJORIE PICKTHALL (1883–1922)

Mercy in Our Time

Let not mistaken mercy
blind my fading sight,
no false euphoria lull me.
I would not unprepared
take this last journey.
Give me a light to guide me
through dark valleys,
a staff to lean upon,
bread to sustain me,
a blessing in my ear
that fear may not assail me.
Then leaving do not hold my hand,
I go to meet a friend —
that same who traced
compassion in the sand.

NANCY HOPKINS

Dancing

Green Dancer

Awaken Spring, Green Dancer,
Dancing Spring of Life.
Greening Love's Joy
In a never ending
Spiral of Light.

Awaken Summer, Green Dancer,
To dance in a world
Greening deep in shades
Of Life's mystery.
Unfolding, enfolding truth.

Awaken Autumn, Green Dancer.
Raising up the falling leaves
In whirlpools of dancing colour.
Brown, red, orange, yellow, olive;
The year's last curtain-call.

Awaken Winter, Evergreen Dancer
With your message of hope.
While nature sleeps, your rhythm
Moves the earth beneath to song,
Of Spring, Summer, Autumn days,
Those passed, and yet to come.

JOAN JOHNSON

God Dances With Us

God, you invite us to dance in delight,
shaping and forming in figures of grace.
We move to the pulse of creation's music
and rejoice to be part of the making of earth.

Praise in the making, the sharing, the moving;
praise to the God who dances with us.

In the steps of Jesus we reach to our partners,
touching and holding and finding our strengths.
Together we move into patterns of freedom,
and rejoice to be part of the sharing of hope.

Praise in the making, the sharing, the moving;
praise to the God who dances with us.

We whirl and spin in the Spirit's rhythm,
embracing the world with our circles of joy.
Together we dance for salvation and justice,
and rejoice to be part of the moving of love.

Praise in the making, the sharing, the moving;
praise to the God who dances with us.

Amen

JAN BERRY

A Blessing on Myself

may the sun be golden on the leaves of my tree
and the flower of the garden be in my hair
the wind on my white linen hung on the line
the babe at my breast, the sweet milk flowing
his father in the house, my true companion
planing the wood or stirring the pot
the bread rising on my own hearth
its smell going out to all my neighbours
and I shall give thanks to the Three and the One
and Mary and Bride my sisters in Christ

VERONICA ZUNDEL

Heaven's Happiness

He said the pleasantest manner of spending a hot July day was lying from morning till evening on a bank of heath in the middle of the moors, with the bees humming dreamily among the bloom, and the larks singing high up overhead . . . That was his most perfect idea of heaven's happiness — mine was rustling in a rocking green tree, with a west wind blowing, and bright white clouds flitting rapidly above; and not only larks but throstles, and blackbirds, and linnets, and cuckoos pouring out music on every side, and the moors seen at a distance, broken into cool dusky dells; but close by great swells of long grass undulating in waves to the breeze; and woods and sounding water, and the whole world awake and wild with joy.

FROM *WUTHERING HEIGHTS*
EMILY BRONTË (1818–48)

The Flame You Light

The flame you light inside me,
Touching a spark to the dry tinder
That was once my heart, is clean and bright,
Awakening the long-lost girl in me
And warming my cold bones.
Drunk with your kisses, rejoicing
In your generous embrace, I feel
Your soft beard on my face
And trace the obvious joy on yours
With unbelieving fingers. I bask,
I bathe in you and press my hungry mouth
To yours again, again, and blaze up
Like a beacon in your arms,
Consumed with pleasure and your tenderness.
My brother, my beloved, cup your hands
Around my heart, shelter me a little
From the wind and keep this flame alight!

ROWENA EDLIN-WHITE

A New Day

The world is clean – washed by the rain,
fresh and new, smelling of
damp earth, green grass and spring;
and I feel as if life were beginning
again for me, that like the
willows, I have renewed my bones
with fledgling leaves. My face
turned upward to welcome the rain;
and I, for all my years, am newly born,
seeing the world with wondering eyes.

MARLA VISSER

*Whatever my age, each day can offer a new beginning. If I turn to welcome it,
it will greet me with infinite possibilities.*

The Grass Is Greenest

In reality, the grass is greenest where we water it most, and there is so
much to live for – if we have the eyes to see – the smile of a small
child, a blaze of colour from a bunch of flowers, or the spontaneous
comment which lifts our spirits and makes us laugh. All are life's gifts
and signs of God's unshakeable commitment to us.

KATHY KEAY

I Am Shaken With Gladness

I am shaken with gladness;
My limbs tremble with joy;
My heart and the earth
Tremble with happiness;
The ecstasy of life
Is abroad in the world.

HELEN KELLER (1880–1968)

I Am the World

I am the song, that rests upon the cloud;
   I am the sun;
I am the dawn, the day, the hiding shroud,
   When dusk is done.

I am the changing colours of the tree;
   The flower uncurled;
I am the melancholy of the sea;
   I am the world.

Am I not one with all the things that can be
   Warm in the sun?
All that my ears can hear, or eyes can see,
   Till all be done.

Of song and shine, of changing leaf apart,
   Of bud uncurled:
With all the senses pulsing at my heart,
   I am the world.

DORA SIGERSON SHORTER (1866–1918)

I Lift the Lord on High

I lift the Lord on high,
Under the murmuring hemlock boughs, and see
The small birds of the forest lingering by
And making melody.
These are mine acolytes and these my choir,
And this mine altar in the cool green shade,
Where the wild soft-eyed does draw nigh
Wondering, as in the byre
Of Bethlehem the oxen heard Thy cry
And saw Thee, unafraid.

FROM *PÈRE LALEMANT*
MARJORIE PICKTHALL (1883–1922)

Jeu d'Esprit

Flame-dancing Spirit, come
Sweep us off our feet and
Dance with us through our days.
Surprise us with your rhythms;
Dare us to try new steps, explore
New patterns and new partnerships;
Release us from old routines
To swing in abandoned joy
And fearful adventure.
And in the intervals,
Rest us
In your still centre.

ANN LEWIN

Bristol, 12th March 1994

Today women will be priested for the first time in England. What joy!
– and after such a struggle. I cannot imagine how it must feel to be one
of them – only that it must be like coming home after a long, tedious,
seemingly never-ending journey. A consummation – a marriage feast –
long withheld. God will be delightedly embodied in these women who
will, for a brief moment, cast off all restraint and celebrate however
they see fit!

And some of us will be there too in the crowds with our children,
who from our earliest years gave ourselves up to be priested
unofficially – willing sacrifices. And we were burnt in the cause as we
offered ourselves time and time again, taking risks, spending our best
energies, being God to the people we were given to serve and bringing
them, hopefully, nearer to God in return.

Many of us, childless by necessity, unnoticed, uncelebrated women
doing our job, fulfilling our ministry, we will be there too, and whilst
we 'whoopee' with our celebrated sisters, we will pray for one another
on the side-lines. Yes, I will pray for all those women whose energies
are still being spent for the cause, who receive little recognition and
even less pay; I will pray for us, that we too will come into our own
and be celebrated, that we too, who have been faithful to the call for
five, ten, twenty years, will have the hard-won freedom through
Christ's battle against all hierarchies, to offer bread and wine to the
hungry.

KATHY KEAY

Exodus

In vibrant celebration
   women dance
   waters dance
celebrating
   community in sisterhood
   solidarity in liberation

Water is Life
women birth Life
Let us celebrate Life
God's gift of liberation!

RANJINI REBERA

Searching

When is the search ended? In one sense, it is finished when our hand, stretched out to God, feels the answering grasp and knows He is there. But in another sense the search never ends, for the first discovery is quickly followed by another, and that by another and so it goes on. To find that He IS is the mere starting point of our search. We are lured on to explore WHAT he is, and the search is never finished, and it grows more thrilling the further one proceeds.

ISOBEL KUHN (1903–57)

Acknowledgements

ALDRIDGE, Susan, 'All the Prodigals are Not Sons' and 'Come Out of the kitchen, Martha' published in *Blooming Women* by the author. Copyright Aldridge. Reprinted by permission of Susan Aldridge.

ASHWIN, Angela, 'Having a Baby – a Parable of Grace' from *Heaven in Ordinary*. Reprinted by permission of McCrimmon Publishing Co. Ltd.

BERRY, Jan, 'God Dances With Us', from *Bread of Tomorrow*, ed., Janet Morley, SPCK.

BOZARTH-CAMPBELL, Alla, 'Affirming the Feminine', an extract from *Womanpriest: a personal odessey*. Reprinted by permission of Paulist Press, USA.

BYRNE, Lavinia IBVM, 'Ministering to Human Need' and 'Naming the Dark Within' from *Sharing the Vision* by Lavinia Byrne. Reprinted by permission of the author.

CAREY, Revd Wendy, 'New Seasons in the Garden'. Printed by permission of Revd Wendy Carey.

CASSIDY, Sheila, 'Lord of the Universe', 'Lord of Creation' and 'Abandonment' all from *Good Friday People*. Reprinted by permission of Darton, Longman & Todd Ltd.

DAVIS, Lucy, 'Leaving Early' and 'She Climbed a Mountain'. Copyright Davis, printed by permission of Lucy Davis.

DE BARY, Anna Bunston, 'Under a Wiltshire Apple Tree', from *The Collected Poems of Anna Bunston de Bary*. Reprinted by permission of Charles Skilton Ltd.

DOBSCHINER, Johanna Ruth, 'Sanctuary', from *Selected to Live*, Marshall Pickering.

DOBSON, Rosemary, 'The Edge', from *Collected Poems*, reprinted by permission of HarperCollins*Australia*; 'Folding the Sheets', from *The Three Fates*, Hale & Iremonger, Sydney, reprinted with permission.

EDLIN-WHITE, Rowena, 'Moel Famau', 'Losing', 'Proposal', 'The Passing of the Foremothers', 'Jesus Taught Us to Pray' and 'The Flame You Light', all copyright Edlin-White and printed by permission of Rowena Edlin-White.

ELDRIDGE-MROTZEK, Maggie, 'A Mother's Prayer for Her Daughter's Baptism', reprinted by permission of Maggie Eldridge - Mrotzek and Revd Gwynfor Evans.

FAINLIGHT, Ruth, 'The Other', from *Selected Poems of Ruth Fainlight*. Reprinted by permission of Sinclair-Stevenson.

FRAME, Janet, 'The Stone', from *An Angel at My Table* and 'Discovery', from *To The Is-land*, HarperCollins.

GUYON, Jeanne, 'A Kind of Prayer', extract from *Exploring the Spiritual Life* ed. Sherwood Eliot Wirt. Reprinted by permission of Lion Publishing plc.

HARDING, Christine and David, 'Grant Us Peace'. Reprinted by permission of Christine and David Harding.

HASKINS, Minnie Louise, 'The Gate of the Year', from *Poetry Please*. Reprinted by permission of Minnie Louise Haskins' Estate.

HOPKINS, Nancy, 'Mercy in Our Time' from *The Lion Christian Poetry Collection* comp. Mary Batchelor. Reprinted by permission of Nancy Hopkins.

INCHFAWN, Fay, 'For a Mercy Received' from *The Journal of a Tent-Dweller* 1931. Reprinted by permission of the publishers, James Clarke & Co. Ltd, Lutterworth Press.

JOHNSON, Joan, 'Green Dancer', copyright Johnson. Printed by permission of Joan Johnson.

JULIAN of NORWICH, excerpts from *The Revelations of Divine Love*, Penguin.

KEAY, Kathy, 'The Womb of God', 'Unnatural Selection', 'Pain and Passion', 'Protest', 'Peace', 'Disillusionment', 'Tragedy', 'A Splash of Colour', 'Visitations', 'Beckoning Grace', 'Choice', 'After Breast Cancer Diagnosis April 1993', 'Bristol, 12th March 1994', unpublished. 'Surviving the Commercial Calendar' from *Letters From a Solo Survivor*; 'Mary Magdalene' from sermon given at Emmanuel College, Cambridge 1991; 'God is With Us' and 'The Grass is Greenest' from 'This is the Day' BBC TV September 1992. All copyright to, and reprinted by permission of the Estate of Kathy Keay.

KELLER, Helen, 'A Little Blind Girl', 'Once in Regions Void of Light' and 'I am Shaken With Gladness', from *The Story of my Life and Letters*, Hodder Headline.

KEMPE, Margery, 'Suffering for Christ', from *The Book of Margery Kempe*, translated by Barry Windeatt (Penguin Classics, 1985), copyright © B. A. Windeatt, 1988.

KNOWLES, Liz, 'Crucifixus Est' from *Christian Thoughts for Everyday*. Reprinted by permission Arrival Press.

KUHN, Isobel, 'Searching' from *By Searching* by Isobel Kuhn. Reprinted by permission of OMF International.

LEVERTOV, Denise, 'O Taste and See' and 'Credo' from *Selected Poems* published by Bloodaxe Books Ltd. Reprinted by permission of Laurence Pollinger Ltd. © 1964 Denise Leverton, *Poems 1960–1967*, reprinted by permission of New Directions Publishing Corp.

LEWIN, Ann, 'Jeu d'Esprit' from *Candles and Kingfishers*. Reprinted permission of Ann Lewin.

METHUEN, Charlotte, 'They Call Me Woman'. Reprinted by permission of Charlotte Methuen.

MOAKES, Margaret, 'To My Mother'. Copyright Moakes. Printed by permission of Margaret Moakes.

MORLEY, Janet, 'Collect for Pentecost' and 'Collect for Lent 1' from *All Desires Known*. Reprinted by permission of Janet Morley.

MOTHER MARY CLARE, 'Listening to God' from *The Little Gidding Anthology of English Spirituality*. Reprinted by permission of Darton, Longman & Todd Ltd.

NICHOLS, Grace, 'Caribbean Woman Prayer', from *Praying with the English Poets*. Reproduced with permission of Curtis Brown Group Ltd., London. Copyright © Grace Nichols, 1990.

PORTLEY, Fran, 'Endurance', from *All the End is Harvest*, Darton, Longman & Todd.

RAINE, Kathleen, 'Message from Home' and 'As You Leave Eden Behind' from *Collected Poems of Kathleen Raine*, HarperCollins.

RATUSHINSKAYA, Irina, 'I Will Live and Survive', reprinted from *No, I'm Not Afraid*, Irina Ratushinskaya, Bloodaxe Books Ltd., 1986.

REBERA, Ranjini, 'Exodus', also 'The Time for Singing Has Come' and 'The Lost Coin', from *The Bible Through Asian Eyes* by Masao Takenaka and Ron O'Grady. Reprinted by permission of Pace Publishing, Auckland, New Zealand, 1991.

RICE, Mary Eleanore, 'A Mother is a Person', from *Images: women in transition*, Upper Room, USA.

ROBINS, Mary, 'May the Wine of the Divine Feminine' from *Desert Flowers*. Reprinted by permission of Cairns Publications.

ROOS, Margaret, 'Meditation on Friendship'. Reprinted by permission of Margaret Roos.

RUDDOCK, Margot, 'Construction', 'O Holy Water', 'Spirit, Silken Thread' and 'Love Song' from *The Lemon Tree* 1937. Reprinted by permission of the publishers, J.M. Dent.

SHAW, Luci, 'With Jacob', from *Postcard from the Shore*, Highland, USA.

SITWELL, Edith, Stanzas 5 & 6 of 'A Love Song' from *Collected Poems* published by Sinclair Stevenson. Reprinted by permission of David Higham Associates.

SMITH, Hannah Whitall, 'Through the Passage Way' and 'Trust', from *A Religious Rebel; the letters of H. W. Smith*, Quakers.

SÖLLE, Dorothee, 'Fear Not' from *Of War and Love*. First published as Im Hause des Menschenfressers: Texte zum Friedan' copyright © 1981 by Rowohlt Taschenbuch Verlag; GmbH, Reinbek bei Hamburg, West Germany. English translation copyright 1983 Orbis Books, Maryknoll, NY 10545. Reprinted by permission.

TAPIA, Elizabeth, 'I Am a Woman', from *No Longer Strangers: A Resource for Women and Worship*, reprinted by permission of World Council of Churches Publications.

UNDERHILL, Evelyn, 'Hope', from *The Wisdom of Evelyn Underhill* and 'Immanence', from *The Oxford Book of Mystical Verse*, Oxford University Press.

VISSER, Marla, 'A New Day', *Images: women in transition*, Highland, USA.

WELBOURNE, Hebe, 'Birth', 'An Icon of Christ's Baptism', 'The Drama of St George', 'On Not Seeing the Kingfisher', 'Prayer', 'Lady in Waiting', 'Laughter' and 'Pembrokeshire Coast Path, August 1989'. Copyright Welbourne. Printed by permission of Hebe Welbourne.

WESLEY, Susanna, 'Be With Me, O God . . .' and 'I Thank Thee, O Lord . . .' from *The Prayers of Susanna Wesley*. Reprinted by permission of Epworth Press.

WILKIE, Ellen, 'Wild Spirit' from *Pithy Poems*. Copyright Estate of Ellen Wilkie. Reprinted by permission of Pauline and John Wilkie.

WILLETTS, Deaconess Phoebe, 'It Takes Two to Share a Vision', 'A Twinkle in God's Eye' and 'Martha and Mary' from *Sharing a Vision*. Reprinted by permission of Revd Alfred Willetts.

WINFIELD, Revd Flora, 'When a Black Woman Decides to Make a Pot', 'A Handful of Clay', 'Anna: a Meditation for Candlemas', 'A Certain Priest, Observed' and 'The Weavers'. Copyright Winfield. Printed by permission of Flora Winfield.

WINTER, Miriam Therese, 'Come Spirit' and 'Take the Time', from *WomanPrayer WomanSong*. Copyright © 1987 by Medical Mission Sisters, Phila., PA 19111. Printed by permission of The Crossroad Publishing Co., NY. [Copyright © 1991 Medical Mission Sisters. Used by permission of the publishers, HarperCollins*Religious*, Australia.]

ZUNDEL, Veronica, 'Orders for an Anchoress', 'God Draws Me', 'Priesthood', 'A Blessing on Myself', 'Song for Kathy' and 'God Speaking'. Copyright Zundel. Printed by permission of Veronica Zundel.

Every effort has been made to trace the ownership of copyright items in this collection and to obtain permission for their use. The compilers and publisher would appreciate notification of, and copyright details for, any instances where further acknowledgement is due, so that adjustments may be made in a future reprint.

Index of First Lines

Index of Authors

Index of Authors —————————————————————— **171**

Laughter, Silence and Shouting

an anthology of women's prayers

COMPILED BY KATHY KEAY

Prayer is honest communication with ourselves and with God. It is not the privilege of the few, but an instinct deep within, needing expression.

Love and friendship, work and home, birth, suffering and the search for life's meaning are some of the themes which have inspired this passionate and beautiful collection of prayers. The contributions are a mixture of the known and much loved prayers of women such as Julian of Norwich and Mother Teresa and the unknown.

Spanning both centuries and continents, they reflect the energy, honesty, hopes and fears of women in every age, from biblical times to the present day.

Laughter, Silence and Shouting will encourage you to pray honestly from the heart and, as you are inspired by the rich variety of images used by others, to write your own prayers. It is as we seek to communicate with ourselves and God in this way that our world, our daily lives and our relationships can be transformed.